MUCH ELSE IN ITALY

By Martin Boyd

Novels

The Langton Sequence :

THE CARDBOARD CROWN

A DIFFICULT YOUNG MAN

OUTBREAK OF LOVE

SUCH PLEASURE

LUCINDA BRAYFORD

NUNS IN JEOPARDY

NIGHT OF THE PARTY

THE PICNIC

THE LEMON FARM

SCANDAL OF SPRING

Autobiography

A SINGLE FLAME

Children's Tale

THE PAINTED PRINCESS

THE FIRST FACE. The Apollo of Veii

Museo di Villa Giulia

MUCH ELSE IN ITALY

*

A Subjective Travel Book

by

MARTIN BOYD

LONDON

MACMILLAN & CO LTD

NEW YORK · ST MARTIN'S PRESS

1958

Copyright © Martin Boyd 1958

MACMILLAN AND COMPANY LIMITED
London Bombay Calcutta Madras Melbourne

THE MACMILLAN COMPANY OF CANADA LIMITED
Toronto

ST MARTIN'S PRESS INC
New York

PRINTED IN GREAT BRITAIN
BY R. & R. CLARK, LTD., EDINBURGH

ACKNOWLEDGMENTS

I must acknowledge my indebtedness to those authors and publishers from whose works I have quoted, and offer my most grateful thanks to Miss Stevie Smith for the motif 'Sweet Cruelty'.

M. B.

Tell me honestly, Socrates, do you believe
this tale of mythology to be true ?

PHAEDRUS

Il faut employer tout pour faire en sorte
que les enfants trouvent la religion belle,
aimable et auguste.

FÉNELON

CONTENTS

ILLUSTRATIONS

CHAPTER I

THE NOUMENA AT PAESTUM

WHEN the train drew out of the station at Paestum and disappeared with its noise towards the south, there fell a blessed silence. After a fortnight in Rome — when even in an inner room, even in the small hours of the morning, the faintly muffled din of the exploding engines of motor bicycles foretold the pandemonium of the coming day — this silence was not merely the absence of sound, but a stillness in which the natural world was eloquent, in which the trees and the stones and the lizards could speak.

In the lane leading from the station to the temples there were many lizards with bright green backs. One ran up a wall, but, when near the coping, fell with a plop into the grass below, disturbing our belief that all natural creatures are perfect in their balance and grace. But this had lost its tail, which may have been due to human agency.

It is May and there are flowers everywhere. Italy is often called the land of flowers. Those who come in the early summer will more easily understand why. In May and June the gardens of Rome fill the air with the scent of all sorts of flowering shrubs, of a kind of laurel with small yellow-green flowers smelling like strong orange blossom, of acacia and lime and jasmine, while the churches, stuffed with lilies, breathe out wafts of perfume into the noisy streets.

Here at Paestum the flowers are more plentiful and more innocent, and the scent is of clover and honeysuckle. Perhaps this abundance of flowers is due to the fact that about 2,000 years ago the mouths of the near-by rivers silted up, and the city and the surrounding plains became a swamp, so that now the earth is very fertile. Corn, scarlet with poppies, is growing beside the lane. In the hedges are mammoth purple thistles mixed with honeysuckle. Along the side of the enclosure of the temples (about ten or more acres) is a hedge of roses, and we enter through a wide parterre of cabbage roses, but these naïve fat flowers are of the modern world. The chicory and vetch beyond might have been woven into the wreaths for the heifers led to sacrifice in these temples, or offered by a boy, with a lock of his hair, to a wayside statue of Hermes. Only three temples remain, and some of those broken foundations which are usually so dull, but here sprouting with yellow and purple vetch, with anchusa, and bright with more lizards.

In the train we had wondered if our first Greek temples would convey to us all that through a lifetime these words had meant to our imagination, if we would breathe the pure serene of Homer's world, or feel the excited reverence with which Goethe, ignoring Cimabue and Giotto, looked on the much less impressive temple of Minerva at Assisi. Would some inadequacy, a lack of scholarship or of aesthetic response, make us unable to say more than, 'It's very interesting to think that they are so old. It is a pity that all the ornament has gone . . .'?

Now only the columns and pediments of warm Travertine rock remain, but originally they were jewels, blazing with colour and carving. Because all that has vanished, we are free to clothe what is left from our imagination, which may not be historically accurate. There never existed a Grecian urn like the subject of Keats's ode, and almost certainly there was not a Greek life like that we imagine here, for we only remember what, from time to time, has seemed most beautiful and wise in the lives of a people who, if they had been driven from Paradise, had not strayed far from the gates. They were still naked and unashamed, and the garlands were still on their heads.

It was not necessary to wonder whether our response

would be adequate. It is automatic. These great skeletons are as immediately impressive as a Gothic cathedral, but more satisfying. They do not try to drag our minds upwards away from the earth, yet they are just as full of mystery — that of our life in its natural setting. They are at peace with the natural world. Some crows circle above the temple of Poseidon, two men are cutting hay amongst the ruins towards the temple of Ceres, and everywhere are the flowers and the lizards. Away to the right are the mountains from which the savage Lucans descended to rape the rich city, in the years before its flood, following what seems to be the law of an inevitable tide. In the plains the people acquire wisdom and create beauty, and the barbarians from the north and from the mountains descend to destroy them. Away to the west, the sea is beyond the fields. Here and there are a few pines and olive trees. The stones give out their emanations, and in this silence, after the fortnight of exploding cylinders, we are receptive to them.

We have been taught about the noumena behind pheno-mena : a noumenon being an object of purely intellectual intuition. As philosophers themselves are not unanimous on the meaning of this word, we may give it our own variation, regarding a noumenon as an idea or spirit that expresses itself in matter ; and though being derived from a passive participle it is an object, we regard it as an active object. The Supreme Noumenon is that object of intuitive apprehension (not to us 'intellectual') which is generally called God. As the word noumenon is in its derivation related to the word Nóos, 'the Active Principle of the Universe',[1] we shall, making the distinction, as it were, between God and the angels, describe this supreme power as the Nóos. Our purpose in using these terms is to free what we believe to be realities from the nauseating associations of the jargon that has been applied to them.

[1] Liddell and Scott.

We have not the learning to distinguish between ideas and spirits. Perhaps they are not distinguishable ; as we have been taught by those who claim to know, that every good thought we have, every virtue we possess, is due to a spirit which is a third part of God. And so we can only call the ideas which come to us here, the spirits which emanate from these ancient stones, the noumena of the temples, of which the proportions follow some subtle mathematical law. The laws of mathematics are eternal. Is that all that satisfies us ? Do they account sufficiently for the visions which fill our minds : of the lowing heifer, of the statue of Hermes 'guarding the lovely playing-grounds. Often boys offer marjoram to me, and hyacinths, and bunches of fresh violets'?[1]

The suggestion that these evocations are due to something beyond matter will not be acceptable to the modern, or perhaps we should say the recent, scientific mind, as pure materialism seems to be already outmoded. There have been experiments in America to do with super-sensory perception and telepathy, and the influence of a person's state of mind on inanimate objects, which appear to have proved the existence of forces of which most people who live at all sensitively have always been aware. Their recognition is becoming more general in the writings of intellectuals, though the experiments and their results have infuriated some scientists who declare : 'Whatever you discover we are committed to a materialistic conception of the universe.' So we find the materialistic scientist at last where he belongs, in the same boat as his ancestor, the puritan fundamentalist. They both suffer from the same vanity, the insistence that they can explain everything ; one by the arbitrary and literal meaning of the words of the Bible, the other by his discovery of the mechanics of nature. They both ignore the vast, mysterious, and unpredictable movement of the noumena. We leave them

---

[1] *Nikias.* 'Poems from the Greek Anthology', tr. Forrest Reid (Faber & Faber).

together, at any rate for the purposes of this book, glaring at each other from opposite ends of their narrow craft, and terrified to move lest it should capsize.

For our purpose is to find the meaning of what we see, not merely to feel the agreeable itching in our finger-tips, by which, Mr. Berenson tells us, we recognize the 'tactile values' in a great work of art. We want as well to become aware of the spirit that possessed the soul of its creator. 'In the great artist', said Turgenev, 'the head and the heart must be equal partners.' [1] Whoever truly sees a picture or a statue must share something of the feeling the artist had in his heart. On the travels which we begin here, sitting on the steps of the temple of Ceres, we are unlikely to look at anything which is not beautiful in its execution, but we are more concerned to recognize the noumena which brought it into being.

But the noumena are vague. They blow where they list, and we cannot hope alone, even in moments of stillness like this, by exposing our sensibility to their influence, to gain any coherent understanding of their purpose. We must take into account the accumulated experience of our race. Whenever they have gathered in their strength and entered the soul of man, forcing him to marvellous expressions of beauty and devotion, they have done so through the medium of a story, and the two stories which in the Western world have coloured our souls are the Greek story and the Christian story. They have made us what we are, or what the best of our kind have been, and they have left some of their richest evidence in Italy. In this country we are plunged into the two stories, and at Paestum we are at the beginning. The intention of our travels is to find the fullest meaning of what we see, not merely to appraise with bleak intellectual eyes the technique of something created with the heart's blood, like the west wall of the Sistine Chapel, where Michelangelo has recorded the sufferings of his life.

[1] *Turgenev*, David Magarshack (Faber & Faber).

Those of us whose schooldays were over by 1914 know our stories. We are inclined to accept them, though with qualifications which are only possible to people of our age. But supposing there is with us a young man who has just come to believe that the spiritual world exists, that there is a force beyond matter but able to control it, how much of our two stories will reveal to him that force, and how much of them will he be able to accept? So on our journey we are accompanied, as it were, by a kind of White Boy in search of God. We had better call him a European boy, of what nationality is not yet certain. He is free of many English prejudices and yet has some English qualities, particularly a love of freedom and justice, but he is more imaginative than most Englishmen. He has not been to a public school and his natural responsiveness has not been conventionalized. But he is anxious to be civilized, and the civilization at which he aims is that described by Mr. Hugh Fausset: 'For what is it to be civilised? It is surely to draw upon inward resources, and at the same time be responsive to one's environment; it is out of the fullness of a true self to respect the uniqueness of every living person or creature, and to be incapable of exploiting them. It is to co-operate with the spirit of nature, rather than to master her physical processes by intellectual cunning, or for selfish ends.'[1] He will also agree with Turgenev: 'This word civilisation is comprehensible, pure and sacred, and the others, such as nationality, glory and so on, smell of blood'.[2]

Perhaps, as it was an Irishman who sent the Black Girl in search of God, it would be just to make this young man an Irish boy, engaged on the same search. He is a Southern Irish Protestant, but with a Catholic sense of poetry, but also with an inherited prejudice against Catholicism, so that what he accepts must result from a conviction that overcomes it.

An Anglican clergyman has referred to 'the Christian

[1] *Poets and Pundits*, Hugh I'A. Fausset (Cape).
[2] *Turgenev*, David Magarshack.

myth'. He did not mean that it was untrue, but that it was the story which clothed the truth. Man cannot possibly understand the full nature of God, the Creative Nóos, for we cannot understand what is greater than ourselves. A dog may know and love his master, but he cannot understand the processes of his mind. So we can only apprehend the Nóos through symbols. Dr. Arnold Toynbee admits that myths 'are indispensable to man for probing a mystery that is beyond his intellectual horizons'.[1] The Christian story, said the Anglican clergyman, is the symbol of our belief. We can accept it as such in its completeness, and live in it ourselves. Sometimes myth and truth fuse together in a moment of light. When this does not happen we may still live in the story, and perceive its truth as through poetry, until the light returns. In the Italian language, history and story are the same word, *storia*. If we live in the Christian story, we live in history, not always of verifiable physical event, but in the history of our own being. The Irish boy wants to discover how much this is possible for himself.

But there are two stories which concern us. We may live in the Christian story, we may accept it in good faith as the symbol of truth, but how can we live in the Greek story ? We find that we have often done so, without any effort of will. The way we have accepted it, without strain or obligation, but from love of its humanity and wisdom and physical grace, is perhaps the way we should have accepted the Christian story. For many people have lived by the Greek story without theological speculation, without hatred and murder resulting from disagreement as to the nature of Zeus, Apollo, and Pallas ; without damning eternally those who did not believe that Pallas sprang from the brain of Zeus, as the Holy Ghost proceeds from the Father.

For the Greek myths, too, were symbols of reality, though

[1] *An Historian's Approach to Religion*, Arnold Toynbee (Oxford University Press).

of less clearly understood reality than the Christian myth. The early Church did not deny the existence of the old gods, but regarded them as evil noumena, as devils. They were not devils but merely unredeemed, and, like mankind, the pagan gods had to be redeemed. Ceres, on whose temple steps — the most beautiful of all — we are sitting, was the spirit which causes the earth to produce corn and fruit and flowers. The chemical processes discovered by the scientists are only the means, not the cause of this growth. The cause they called Ceres, as Christians call it God the Father. The noumena, whatever they have been named, must use material processes to create material phenomena. The scientist has only discovered the processes and does not want to be bothered with the meaning. It reduces his cleverness, for he can only discover fact. To discover the truth behind it, he would need aesthetic and spiritual apprehensions, which he is unlikely to have, or he would not be a scientist, at least not one solely concerned with phenomena. M. Jacques Maritain, who believes that Descartes originated this divorce of science from truth, has written : 'Cartesian evidence . . . mechanises nature, it does violence to it ; it annihilates everything which causes things to symbolise with the spirit, to partake of the genius of the Creator, to speak to us. The universe becomes dumb.' [1] Incidentally, this scientific violence to nature, originally an idea, has now achieved its physical phenomenon. Or we may quote from the opposite pole. D. H. Lawrence wrote of a young German scientist who would allow no meaning to the Etruscan art which they saw together : 'He is a scientist, and when he does not want anything to have meaning, it is *ipso facto* meaningless'.[2] Lawrence may not be so far from M. Maritain as we think. They both seek life made whole, but Lawrence looked no farther than the Apollo of Veii.

And so those gods, too, have meaning. Apollo is the

---

[1] *The Dream of Descartes*, Jacques Maritain (Nicholson & Watson).
[2] *Etruscan Places*, D. H. Lawrence (Secker).

source of all our light and beauty, and Latona, like the Blessed Virgin, could find no place for his birth. Hermes is the noumenon behind all that swift movement, both of body and mind, which is most evident in youths, so that it is to him that the boys offer their sprigs of marjoram, and when their boyhood is past, their relinquished toys, their tops, and boxwood rattles. He is the patron of travel and letters, and also, because he is unredeemed, of liars and thieves. Poseidon, whose temple, circled by crows, is a quarter of a mile away across the sprouting ruins, is the noumenon of the sea, of elusive influence and treachery, but also of that inspiration which has a mysterious beauty, like the effects of light on water, or through cloud and steam. All the gods have meaning, and what has meaning exists.

The correspondences which we may note between the Greek, or any other, and the Christian myths, do not weaken the authority of the latter, but strengthen it immensely, by showing that it corresponds with what is profound and eternal in the human soul, and that in the beginning was the Nóos — the Logos which was God.

Apart from this, the Greek story has formed to a great extent the soul of the Western world, of the race to which the Irish boy belongs, and he must include it in the region of his search for his god, the nóos which will illuminate his own heart and mind. It has been said : 'You cannot build a tree'. Culture, which must include a religion, is a growth, and you cannot make a 'culture' in a generation. By this word we do not mean the aesthetic appreciations of a small clique, but the spirit that possesses a whole people. If the Irish boy, who is also part of our own mind, is to find the correspondence to his soul, which is already formed, it must be in those two stories which have formed it — which contain the noumena of beauty, truth, and goodness, worshipped by those of his race, as Apollo, Pallas-Athene, and Zeus, and more clearly as the Son, the Holy Ghost, and the Father ; while Ceres, the

B

fruitful mother of the corn, which redeemed became the Body of Christ, was known in the Eleusinian mysteries only by a name signifying sorrow, the *Mater Dolorosa*.

He does not need to be a classical scholar to do this, any more than one needs to be a theologian to be a Christian. Keats had little more Greek learning than he gleaned from the Classical Dictionary. The Irish boy's search will be conducted more with the heart and the eye than with the intellect, and his prayer to the noumena of the temples, before we leave the enclosure to set out on our pilgrimage, will be that of Socrates : 'O Blessed Pan and all spirits dwelling in this place, grant that I may be beautiful in the inner man, and that what I have of outer things may accord with those that are within'. It is possible that at the end of his search he will add 'per Christum Dominum nostrum', but this we do not yet know, and on our pilgrimage we are essentially free-thinkers.

Even so, we shall be living largely in the Christian story. It will be the provisional symbol of our belief. At times, using its language, we may speak of what are only symbols as if they were actualities. As we have said, the instruments of our search are the heart and the eye, and we have no certainty where is the exact borderline between the truth and the symbol.

After these considerations we were ready to move. We stood up, stretched ourselves, and walked back through the stones and the lizards, the vetch and the anchusa, and the par-terres of fat cabbage roses, out of the precincts of the temples.

Across the road, nearly opposite the temple of Ceres, is the new museum, built to house the Etruscan remains — vases on which the figures have those strange smiling faces showing perfect satisfaction with their physical life. The full smiling mouth is most clearly seen in the statue of Zeus, the same kind of mouth which we saw later in the Apollo of Veii. The temple of Poseidon was possibly Etruscan, and this face is the phenomenon into which the noumena of the place forced material substance. This Zeus, with what is left of his face, looks on the natural world with complete approval. The belief that, though imperfect, it is essentially good, is one that the Irish boy holds and will never give up. He accepts both the view of this Zeus and the first condition of the Christian story, that the Creative Nóos looked on the world and 'saw that it was good'.

There are two other things in this museum which here first drew his attention. They are the winged boy, and the boy on a dolphin. We find the winged boy wherever we go in Italy, though not always with wings. He is the everlasting child, the *putto*, adored of the Italians. Apparently nothing can take place without him. At the seduction of Danae he is playing in the corner ; at the martyrdom of S. Peter he is waiting cheerfully with the palm and the crown for the last agonies of the saint to end ; at the Dispensation of the Blessed Sacrament he is unconcerned at the feet of Almighty God. He is also gambling in the streets.

The boy on the dolphin, too, expresses something which is an element in our search, and that is our freedom in the natural world. It is the supreme expression of humanity abandoned in ecstasy to the rhythms of nature. For whoever can ride on a fish is free from all the trammels that humanity has known, so that the boy on the dolphin is a symbol, perhaps of man before the Fall, or of the human soul escaped to freedom.

CHAPTER II

AMALFI

WE had planned an ordinary holiday, but now the influence
of the temples had made us turn it into a kind of search or
pilgrimage. We did not, because of this, change the plan of
our journey and follow a different route, and so, though most
of what we record will be relevant to our search, there will be
interludes of necessary relaxation. This applied most to the
fortnight after we left Paestum. We had to find our direction.
Within those walls the universe was limited and in harmony
with itself. The Etruscan face was not troubled by doubt or
a sense of guilt, and the Greeks were still close to the gates of
Paradise. The Irish boy had to conduct his search in a much
more complicated world.

A young man in the train pointed out the military
cemeteries which we passed, and spoke of the shelling of
Salerno. We said that it was wicked to choose Italy, the
mother of our civilization, as the battlefield between England
and Germany. His eyes flashed and he said that it was wicked
to choose any country anywhere as a battlefield.

At Salerno we went to see the cloisters and strange tower
of the cathedral, which startled us slightly. They are outside
the scope of our search, Norman or Arabian with their striped
and pointed arches. An importunate guide kept repeating,
'Without me you may miss something'. We could not
explain to him that on our travels we intended to miss a great
deal; all that was irrelevant to our mood, however historic or
beautiful those things might be. We did not want our minds
to become a confused jumble of unrelated images. We
escaped from him into the cathedral, where there are two of

12

those superb twelfth-century mosaic pulpits, and two beautiful tombs, one of Margaret of Anjou, on which are the ubiquitous lilies of France, flowering in patches all over Europe, from here to the gateways of Cambridge colleges. There are also large expanses of newly plastered wall, the repair of war damage. An English gentlewoman was looking at these with approval : 'The bombing has been a great improvement to Italy,' she said. 'It's cleared away so much of the rubbish that was in these churches.'

We went on to Amalfi, fourteen miles along that coast road, where the bus-drivers, with their nonchalant skill and good-tempered patience, see-saw their huge vehicles round hair-pin bends at the edges of a precipice. At Amalfi we returned to a paradise, but a different one, not of classical serenity and animal innocence, but of medieval imagination. That mountain-side, we should have thought, could only exist in the dreams of Perugino. The piled-up labyrinth of houses culminates in the little baroque tower of S. Biagio. Behind it are the terraces of vines, the dark spires of a pair of cypresses, escarpments, more vines and trees, and small white houses or ruined towers perched on inaccessible crags. From the rocks come cascades of flowers, valerian and honeysuckle, and above are the aerial mountains. One of the characteristics of the modern world is cowardice in the face of beauty, and ourselves infected by the disease, at the first impact of this vision, could only exclaim 'Great Scott!' Cowardice in the face of heavenly gifts is more evil than cowardice in the face of the enemy, and, perhaps because we have been touched by the influences of virtue at Paestum, we were a little ashamed of our response.

In this fantastic scene we were in the thick of the Christian story. In every direction we are faced with its evidence, though some of it is rather peculiar. In the piazza at the foot of the great flight of cathedral steps is a renascence fountain, a marble Aphrodite from whose breasts spurt twin jets of water, but these have been cruelly mutilated and fitted with brass nozzles, while the marble group itself has been used as a base for a statue in rougher stone of S. Andrew with his cross. The *putti* drink from the fountain as unconcernedly as if it were a chromium-plated tap.

This fountain is an object lesson to us. We have agreed that the pagan gods, which are to some extent our own natures, must be redeemed. Where the Christian religion spreads over the world it has to redeem the gods of the different countries, and the degree of their civilization depends on the nature of these local gods. In Italy they are those of classical times, those we love most, the nearest to the gates of Paradise. Christianity superimposed on these gives a religion of un-bounded richness, Catholic and pagan. In contrast, Calvinism superimposed on some brutish northern gods produces a barren hell. But Christianity must redeem the pagan gods, not merely be superimposed, as this crude statue on the delicate marble of Aphrodite, leaving it still there, but degraded and mutilated. The fountain shows what we must avoid.

Perhaps, before we go any farther, we had better glance at the Christian story. Although the Irish boy had sat through countless recitals of Anglican matins, he had not a very clear idea of the basic design of Western religion, so we attempted a summary.

The world and its inhabitants of every kind were created by the Supreme Nóos, called God the Father, who loved what he had made. Man and the animals lived happily in this world, following the instinct implanted by their creator. But man allowed his intellect and his curiosity to exploit his sensuality, which distorted his nature, so that he lost the per-fection and integrity of being, which on their level is still retained by the animals. So God sent that part of himself which was Beauty, to show mankind how they might live again under the law of innocence, and their redemption began. But at this they were filled with the rage of Caliban, not

seeing his own face in the glass, and they destroyed the body
in which that part of God had clothed himself. In this
destruction his splendour was fully declared, for evil is most
often defeated by the willing suffering of the innocent, not to
gratify the nostrils of a savage god, but because the war still
continues in heaven, in the spiritual world. God has not yet
won. The Son of God returned to his Father, who was also
himself, but he sent to mankind that other part of himself
which was Truth, so that men might know of their redemption, and to comfort them he said that when they ate and
drank their eternal natural food of corn and wine, they would
receive himself. In this his incarnation is repeated, and the
process of redemption continued, for it depends on the descent
of the spirit into matter, on the illumination of the substance
of this world, so that the corn of Ceres becomes the body of
Christ.

This story corresponds with man's own experience on
earth. He begins in the family, which is the centre and symbol
of the Christian religion. He finds that the whole process of
his life is the dying to one condition to fulfil another. He must
give up his pleasure in his existence as a boy to become a man.
A girl must sacrifice her particular grace to become a mother,
and always after the sacrifice is a richer reward. If the Christian myth had no historical foundation at all — an impossible
supposition — it would still remain a deep spiritual truth.
Religious teaching is always half poetry, particularly that in
the gospels, and the disfiguration of Christianity results largely
from the poetry being accepted as fact by literal Western
minds. If we accept the story as the symbol of our spiritual
life, as a poetic, if not always historical, explanation of a
condition, we are not afraid of its minor discrepancies.

Also, as we have already seen, the fact that elements of the
story are found in pre-Christian myths reinforces rather than
weakens its truth. Apollo underwent purification after slaying
Python, and so acquired a redemptive function, and was able

to cleanse from sin. The rites of Adonis, celebrated at Byblus in the spring, were concerned with death and resurrection, and the mourning was for the cruel treatment of the corn by the reaper, and this foreshadows the sacrifice of the corn, the holy bread of Christ's body. These symbols are eternal in the human mind. Or we may say that the Supreme Nóos, groaning and travailing to create the conditions for the Incarnation, gave imperfect indications beforehand — rough sketches of his intention — until in the fullness of time it became the perfect achievement. The vast processes of creation and redemption are not as concise and tidy as the theologians would have us believe. God, if alive, cannot be static. He may be subject to growth, equally with his creation. That he existed before all time may be true, but it is pure speculation. Man's limited brain cannot have any conception of God's full nature and origins. It can only accept a story of them as a working symbol. Except where he is revealed to us through the natural world and through his son, the deeper mysteries of his being are irrelevant to us. This may be amateur theology, but how can anyone have a professional knowledge of God ?

If a man fully understood God, his mind would burst. He can have a professional knowledge of what other men have thought of God, and it is within the limits of what other men have thought that the Irish boy will conduct his search. The professional theologian demands that we should accept his interpretation on his exclusive authority, but the Irish boy reserves the right first to inspect what he is asked to accept. Believing, as he does, that the truth is more often expressed in poetry than in explicit statement, he regards the theologians as unsatisfactory exponents of the story of which they are the often uncomprehending custodians. He realizes that it must have custodians, that its rites must be celebrated, and that it is no use saying : 'I believe that the noumena exist, and that they are the most powerful influences in our lives', without

trying to discover how they act towards him, and how those
who claim to have the greatest knowledge of the subject
believe that they act. Having clarified to this extent our
attitude, we were free once more to look about us.

Two days after our arrival was the feast of Corpus Christi,
when the corn, grown in the fields of Ceres, is consecrated to
become the body of Christ. When the mass was over in the
cathedral, where the columns from Paestum are concealed
beneath baroque ornament — again the pagan beneath the
Christian — a procession was formed. It was led by little
girls from five to eight, dressed as blue angels. Behind them
were elder girls dressed as brides. Next were boys in white
jerseys and blue shorts, then young men in white jerseys and
blue trousers. Then came the acolytes and the clergy, the bishop
carrying the Host under a plumed pink canopy. The brides
and the acolytes carried baskets of flowers, yellow broom,
roses, and field daisies. The rest carried lighted candles,
though they may blow out in the street.

As the procession began to move, the strong, soft Italian
voices broke into the *Pange Lingua*, the hymn which declares :

> Et antiquum documentum
> Novo cedat ritui.

Here this superseding of the past seems to apply not only
to the savagery of the Old Testament, but also to the Greek
story. The blue angels led the way down the great eleventh-
century flight of steps. In the piazza where S. Andrew stands
above Aphrodite — though it is from her mutilated breasts
that the *putti* still draw the water of their physical lives — the
flowers are thrown in the path of the Host. A few yellow
petals fall on the canopy, and stick in the acolytes' hair. Here
and there bowls of hot charcoal are placed at the doors of
shops. The owner flings in a handful of incense and then runs
upstairs to throw flowers from the upper windows. When the
procession turns into the street above the sea, everybody — the

shopkeepers, the fishermen, their wives, the young men at the petrol pumps — stands quietly, and as the canopy passes they kneel to the God who gives meaning to their daily bread, and who feeds the life of their souls. They are living in the story.

If the Materialistic Scientist and the Protestant Fundamentalist in their narrow craft are floating out there on the Catholic sea, they must be horrified at this scene. To the latter it is idolatry, something to be destroyed with that Old Testament savagery which is his true religion. To the former it is simply meaningless. To him the universe is dumb.

The Irish boy, on the other hand, was deeply moved, though his reaction may have been largely aesthetic. He saw that the Amalfitani are living in the story, and not only during this procession. They do it all the time. Two boys walked into the church by the post office. They crossed themselves and walked out again. They seemed to do it from an unconscious impulse, to keep in touch with their noumena. In the same church a woman was teaching her chortling baby to wave to the statue of the Virgin. A daisy was stuck between the feet of a crucifix, as a sprig of marjoram was stuck between the feet of Hermes by the boys of Leonidas.

The cathedral cloisters are called 'The Cloisters of Paradise'. They have the same interlaced arches as those of Salerno, but because of the absence of stripes are less exotic. Here two schoolboys asked us if we were French, as they were going in for a competitive examination in which French was a subject. In spite of our disclaimers they chose to act as our guides, one chattering French and the other Italian in a confusing babel, but somehow the god Hermes, so potent at their age, enabled understanding to pass between us. They led us up some stairs where apparently they had no business to be, as seeming guilty and amused they poked their noses into various official-looking rooms. At the foot of the stairs was a fourteenth-century bas-relief of the Virgin and Child. They crossed

themselves but went on chattering, explaining that it was the
Madonna, much as they might have pointed out in their homes
the portrait of a kind relative. They said good-bye, shaking
hands and bowing with great courtesy, but a few minutes
later met us again and asked, still with princely manners, if we
could *per piacere* possibly give them two cigarettes.

They, too, were living in the story, but with the lightness
proper to their years. Supposing, according to the materialist
sitting out there in his narrow boat, that it is all untrue, that
the Madonna is a myth in the full meaning of the word, and he
can sweep it all away. Will he be satisfied, when he has done
so, that there is no truth missing in the vacuum that follows ?
Again we may turn to M. Maritain, who writes : 'Man is
only a rough sketch drawn by night of his true self'.[1] These
people who kneel to the God who was made man, who wave
to the Madonna, are aware of the existence of the Perfect
Drawing, and because they feel it is always close at hand, they
are consoled for the imperfection of their own features. Would
it advance truth to remove this conception from their minds,
to take them out of the story, and reduce them to organisms
without meaning or direction ?

It is true that there are some ways of living in the story
which are disconcerting to those brought up with Protestant
ideas of reverence, though it is possible that Protestant reverence may be largely evidence of doubt. We hold a fragile
vase gingerly, and put it on a high shelf.

We went to a low mass in the cathedral. The two acolytes
were about eight years old, and wore shorts and open shirts.
Another ran in to join them, but they pushed him away, and
he knelt at the far end of the altar. Then a fourth came and
there was a further scuffle. The moment of Consecration
approached, when all mortal flesh must keep silence.

The *putti* are squabbling as to who shall lift the priest's
chasuble at this supreme moment. One slaps the hand of

[1] *The True Humanism,* Jacques Maritain (Bles).

another who tries to take it. The priest must know what is
happening, but he continues in calm preoccupation with the
mass. They do not disturb him. They are simply the *putti*,
inevitable and essential in any Italian scene, loved and allowed
anywhere, and if they act according to their natures on the
altar steps, it is only to be expected. Their presence there is no
more unsuitable than if they played in a room where their
parents were talking.

The Irish boy can accept them, but he will meet greater
difficulties in his attempt to adjust himself to the story. One
morning we awoke at dawn and looked out on the fantastic
Perugino beauty, the ruins on their crags, the cypresses, the
terraces of vines, and the tower of S. Biagio. Above the
Cappuccini convent the rock face glowed orange, and the pearl-
grey mists were flushed with rose, as if Aphrodite Anadyomene
might soon be born. The cathedral bells rang in a curious
way, first an urgent busy monotone, about two strokes to a
second, then a harsh clanging, the sort of noise one imagines
they made when the Saracen ships were sighted.

Because so often in our lives we have seen reproductions
of water-colours of that Cappuccini convent, now an hotel, we
decided to go up there to tea. The Franciscan convent on
the eastern promontory is also an hotel, and in its beautiful
cloisters rich Protestant tourists take their coffee where the
Franciscans meditated on the beauty of poverty. The chapels
remain as in times past, and in them mass is said every Sunday
for the benefit of the tourists.

The Cappuccini convent is like many things first seen from
below or from afar. The romance evaporates on close in-
spection. The cloisters are poor compared with those of the
Franciscan Hotel Luna, but there is a magnificent pergola, a
place for those who like sitting above the world rather than in
it. Amalfi is not for those who dislike heights. One's inside
dissolves as children leap on to a two-foot wall, which on the
other side drops a hundred feet to the jagged rocks of the sea.

Fat men sleep on these perches after lunch. As we descended from the Cappuccini convent we had that comfortable feeling which we have when the wheels of an aeroplane touch the ground.

The past of Italy exists not only in its architecture and cinquecento landscapes, but in the people themselves. The streets are full of Leonardo models. Mr. E. M. Forster has written of 'The Face of Italy', though he has put a southern Italian face in Tuscany. Descending from S. Biagio, we met one, but this was a Tuscan face in the south. Many southern Italian faces are round, sometimes appearing almost broader than their length, and framed in a circle of dark hair. Their eyebrows are semicircles and their eyes are round. They are friendly, but they do not easily smile, perhaps because they are lazy and it needs an effort to force this round composure, these faces formed in the symbol of eternity, into a different pattern. For that is the effect of their smiles, of a changed pattern, not of an extension of the inherent design. Perhaps the true face of Italy is a blending of the different types. One of the finest examples is that of S. Pius X, though he had a German surname. It is not beautiful in the way that the faces of our illustrations are beautiful. It is a more earthly face than any of them, even than the Apollo of Veii. It is the face of a peasant, but the spirit shines through its earthliness and so it is a pure expression of the Christian religion. He died of a broken heart at the outbreak of the 1914 war. His enormous shoes, made for his peasant's feet, but embroidered with gold, are in his chapel in S. Prassede on the Esquiline hill, near the fragment of the column to which Christ was tied for the scourging.

The face we met below S. Biagio was pure Leonardo, and belonged to a girl of sixteen. She asked if we would like to see the view from the tower. She led us up some steps and opened the door of a small panelled chapel, full of women chanting vociferously.

'Maddalena,' she called to one of them ; 'Inglesi.'

Maddalena left her stall, and still chanting as if she were wound up and unable to stop, came out to us.

'Come this way, please,' she said. 'Ave Maria, gratiae plena, Dominus tecum.'

'Please don't let us disturb your devotions,' we begged, horrified at our intrusion.

'Come this way,' she repeated, and led the way farther up the stone stairs, chanting 'Benedicta tu in mulieribus, et Benedictus Fructus ventris tui'.

From somewhere came one of those unfortunate smells so frequent in Mediterranean ports. The girl said 'Phoo', and held her Leonardo nose, which we were glad to find was as sensitive as it was beautiful.

We arrived on a balcony above the chapel. The girl said : 'Bella veduta.' Maddalena sang determinedly : 'Sancta Maria, Mater Dei, ora pro nobis, nunc et in hora mortis nostri'.

It was a beautiful view. The afternoon sunlight was on the old pale stone of the Franciscan convent, on the towers, the crags and the mountains above the purple sea. Honeysuckle, yellow broom, and valerian hung from the rocks above us, but we could not enjoy it under the loud reproach of Maddalena's chanting. Was she gaining an indulgence by it, 500 days off Purgatory, and therefore must not stop ? Were we the possible cause of 500 days of torment for the unfortunate woman ? Even if indulgences were pure superstition, if she believed in them, if they are part of her story, at least we might be disturbing her peace of mind.

We admired the view as hurriedly as possible and returned down the stone stairs. Maddalena's voice was reunited to the formidable drone in the chapel. We only gave her 50 lire because we did not quite approve of her leaving it. We gave the Leonardo girl 100 lire because of her lovely face, and went on down to the beach to bathe.

There is always some drama going on amongst the *putti*

on the beach, and also higher up on the terrace, where there is an attempt to give the effect of a smart café, with shaded lamps on the tables. Here they seat themselves as unconcernedly as they squabble on the altar steps. Occasionally one of them will abandon the stage they have made of all the world they know, to ask for *dieci lire*. If this is refused they ask for *cinque lire*, and if this is refused they smile indifferently and return to the drama of their lives.

One hears much disapproving comment on the begging in southern Italy. In Naples, two undergraduates stopped in a side street and took out their limited money, to see how much they could afford for lunch. It was not much, but to some children who saw them it was great riches. They clamoured around them and the noise drew more, until there were fifty children shouting for money. The undergraduates ran for it, and took refuge in one of those restaurants where there are also piles of fruit and cheese and other food. The children stormed the restaurant, the oranges and the *bel paese* rolled on the floor, and amidst the wreckage the waiters had to drive them out with brooms. This is an extreme example of begging which we can hardly commend, but a country where there are poor, but no beggars, is not Christian. Begging blesses him that gives and him that takes. The beggar demands recognition of our common humanity, and when we give to him we acknowledge it. Where begging is forbidden it is only so that the rich may not be disturbed in the enjoyment of their wealth. When, in Protestant countries, we remove the beggars with the crucifixes from the street corners, we are more comfortable. That is our virtue.

There is a sort of counterpart to the begging. There is not enough work and half the young men who spend the day bathing, or doing something with boats, are unemployed. We asked what they lived on and were told, quite casually, as if it were not at all strange, that those who are employed share their wages with those who are not. So these ordinary young

men have achieved what is the first principle of pure Christianity, the one that could save the world. They love their
neighbours as themselves. They have rejected the worship
of the Golden Calf, which is destroying our civilization. In
all our time in Italy, in fact in our whole lives, we have seen
nothing more remarkable, no one whose shoes we were less
worthy to untie, than these young men who do not regard
the fruits of their labour as exclusively their own.

One evening after dinner we were invited by an English
couple from the Franciscan hotel to have coffee at one of the
smart tables amongst which the *putti* were pretending to be
trains. They had brought two other English people from the
hotel, an apparently rich man and his wife, who often made
long motoring tours in Italy. We said how considerate it was
of the beggars to ask for *dieci lire*, stating exactly what they
wanted, and so saving us from either extravagance or mean-
ness. One only needed to walk about with a pocket full of
light aluminium coins. The rich man was furious. 'I never
give anybody anything', he declared righteously, elevating
his tight fist into an ornament of virtue. After that he turned
his back on us and talked to his host about cricket, his integrity
unsullied by a gift to Christ's poor children. They may only
want it to play their gambling game, a kind of dim relation to
bowls, which if they have no *dieci lire* they play with the tops
of mineral-water bottles. If they do, does it matter ? The rich
man probably plays bridge and he and his wife must be spend-
ing over 10,000 lire a day on their tour, though they pay
nothing for all that they see outside of museums, the Perugino
hillside and the wine-dark sea. But it would be an act of
blasphemy against the Golden Calf, their true god, to give
one-thousandth of what they daily spend on themselves to
a child whose country this is, and whose poverty is often
terrible.

Here we may refer to a part of the story which is relevant
to our search. The three temptations in the wilderness repre-

sent the three stages of sin into which we may fall. The first is simply to gratify physical appetites, to turn the stones into bread. The sins of the flesh are comparatively trivial and easily forgiven. The next temptation, more serious, is to obtain and exercise power, to accept the offer of the kingdoms of the world. The third temptation, the greatest of all, is to spiritual pride. Throw yourself down and you will exhibit yourself as miraculously supported by angels. We may say very roughly that the Catholic Church has fallen most to the first two temptations and the Protestant to the third. The puritan plunges straight into the third temptation, and in his last horrible manifestation, the rich business man, in pride of his righteousness he refuses a penny to the poor children of Christ.

The Irish boy, who is aware of the temptations of the flesh and feels that they may prevent his accepting life in the story, is glad to know that they are the most easily forgiven. After all he was created by the Supreme Nóos, who planted in him lively appetites. In former times he could have married at eighteen or twenty, and could reasonably have been asked to remain chaste until that age. But can he be expected to do so until thirty or more, when he may be able to afford to marry? Again is not chastity a purely negative virtue, allowing a mystic to devote his whole impulse towards the Absolute, and the priest to avoid worldly entanglements? Is it a virtue at all to anyone who intends to be neither a mystic nor a priest?

The young Catholic Amalfitani live in the story, but they do not look very chaste. At least their faces are not disfigured by the bleak lines of puritanism. How do they manage? Is it because their priests know the order of the temptations, and regarding the sins of the flesh as trivial, accept with a mild rebuke that man must live according to his nature; knowing, too, that whoever from love rather than obligation shares with his penniless brother cannot be in much sin.

c

The next day we went up to Ravello, see-sawing round the hair-pin bends above the precipices, and we entered an even more fantastic extension of the beauty of Amalfi. The towers and convents perch on more impossible crags. The sunlight streamed through the green of the walnut trees which flank the road and, when we arrived in the piazza, in through the wide-open cathedral doors. Here, unexpectedly, is something we had always wanted to see, but had forgotten its whereabouts — the magnificent coloured mosaic pulpit, mounted on six columns, each of which is supported on the back of a small walking lion. We do not know whether there is any symbolism in these lions, or whether they are just sheer fun. But in nearly all great art is there not an element of sheer fun ? Except perhaps in Protestant art, because Protestants do not accept or do not emphasize the Incarnation. For those who love the natural world — and every true artist, like God, the Supreme Nóos, or the Zeus of Paestum, must love creation — are unable to resist adorning what they make, even if the adornment is inconsequent. Though we cannot be certain that these inconsequent little lions have no meaning.

Through the sleepy sunlit afternoon we floated about in a medieval dream. There is a walnut tree in a little cornfield, below which the hill descends a thousand feet to the sea, and on a stone across the road S. Francis sat to meditate. Wagner composed *Parsifal* in the Villa Rudolfo, and its magic garden became Klingsor's. It is impossible to exaggerate the beauty of Ravello. When the inhabitants descend to the ordinary world, rich in colour and history as it is in their neighbourhood, they must feel that they have fallen from Eden. Yet it was in this heavenly place that the Irish boy had his first touch of misgiving. Under the altar of the cathedral is a vessel containing the blood of S. Pantaleone, martyred under Diocletian. It liquefies every year on the twenty-seventh of July.

When he came up against something of this kind he was inclined to slacken his search, and spend his time on the beach, where the *putti* pursue their day-long drama, until, hours after sunset, they seek their beds somewhere in the piled-up labyrinth below S. Biagio, as mysterious to us as the secret haunts of wild creatures in a wood, and there they dream of their friends' faces against the sea, and of hands full of *dieci lire*.

On the beach a boy of about fifteen had a *putto* a few years younger in his grasp. He was like a puppy with a ball. He flung him into the sea, then, pretending not to notice that he had crept out, suddenly flung him in again. They were both very amused. Soon the small boy became rather tired, but the big boy went on with the game. At the small boy's age we would have been blind with anger, and used any weapon to defend ourselves, but he continued to endure the treatment with a faint smile of good-humour and patience. His features were fine and sensitive and he gave the impression of being infinitely civilized. We met him again, twenty-three years older.

On our last day at Amalfi we went again to the cathedral, to see the tomb of S. Andrew, whose body was brought here from Constantinople in A.D. 1208. On the wall of the staircase is a fourteenth-century crucifix, of which the face is neither suffering nor sentimental, and for this reason attracted the notice of the Irish boy, who had unconsciously begun to look for the face which might be that of the Perfect Drawing. The figure has at one time been gilded, but is now only flecked with gold, which gives it a faintly luminous appearance. Under the altar in the crypt, which was decorated at the expense of Philip II of Spain, are the bones of the saint. Every year on his festival they give out a miraculous fluid called 'the manna of S. Andrew'. It is kept in a sealed container and, sprinkled on cotton wool, will be given to visitors on application to the archbishop's secretary.

Again the Irish boy receives a slight jolt. We explained to him that these local miracles are excrescences on the story and do not have to be accepted. He asked if the archbishop's secretary believes in this disagreeable phenomenon. We could not say, but even if he did not, he could not suddenly declare to simple people that they had been hoaxed. There might be a root that had thrust its way into the foundations of our house. If we pulled it out suddenly the wall might collapse.

We only stayed ten days at Amalfi, as it did not seem the kind of country in which the Irish boy could profitably conduct his search, and yet he received there the basic impression without which all that might follow would be merely useless stimulation of his sensibility — the impression of humanity. For humanity is the basis of the Christian story. Its theology is entirely concerned with man and his needs, and its central belief is that God became man, to show us how to live in innocence. The Christian story, which from now on we shall mean when we mention simply 'the Story', corresponds, as we have seen, with the experience of human life. One of the phenomena of our times is the distortion of the meaning of words. Hermes, riotous and unredeemed in the daily papers, creates senseless phrases to confuse virtue or disguise truth. On wireless programmes we hear debates between Christians and 'Humanists', the latter generally atheist. But apart from the great classicists to whom this description truly belongs, and who would look with astonished Olympian contempt at the sterile materialists who claim the description today, it is impossible to be a humanist and to ignore the noumena. We should have thought it was also impossible to be a true scientist. The Christian story most clearly emphasizes the value of the individual human soul, which distinguishes us essentially from the animals, though who can say that noble and faithful animals have no place in paradise? The 'scientific-humanist' who treats man as a phenomenon without a noumenon would only be justified in calling himself a 'scientific-animalist'. But man, as is very evident, has become distorted, he is out of drawing, whereas the animals retain on their level their innocence and perfection of being. So the scientific-materialist who has lost his perfection but who denies the soul would only be justified in calling himself a 'scientific-sub-animalist', a good enough name for those who can use theories evolved in the degraded hell where Pavlov tortured his dogs.

The first thing the Irish boy had to do was to get rid of these false conceptions planted in his mind by the unredeemed Hermes, and to recover his feeling of humanity. There could be no better place to do so than in Italy. From it comes our Christian and our classical humanism. Each European has his fatherland, but for every civilized man in the Western world, Italy must be his motherland, as a child most often owes its greatest gifts of life and its finest teaching to its mother. Here the basic patterns and feelings of our civilization continue. When the young men down among the boats, or the woman making fishing-net bags below the hotel, break into song, it is not into jazz, but into some air that seems to breathe the ancient sorrows and passions of humanity. With the Italians the heart comes first and the intellect second, which we believe is the right order. Certainly the Irish boy can only hope to find his nóos with his heart, as he has no great intellectual pretensions, though he has enough sense to know that, however great his endowments, if he understood God his mind would burst. Therefore Amalfi, where there is so much humanity, where the young men share their earnings with the hungry, where the *putti* play both amongst the smart café tables and on the altar steps, seemed as good a place as any to begin his pilgrimage. When we drove away, half a dozen friends whom we had made in those few days waved to us with that curious beckoning motion, which seems more to be calling one back than saying good-bye.

★

We had intended to leave Amalfi by the steamer which leaves daily for Naples, calling at Capri on the way, but on

that day the sea became very rough ; the steamer, as it floated
by the quay, appeared very restive and mobile ; and there
seemed to be no reason, except for a glimpse of Capri, to
endure the equivalent of four hours' channel crossing when it
was possible to go by train from Salerno.

Two years ago, at Cava di Tirreni, set in a romantic valley,
there was a landslide. The fallen earth mixed with the swollen
torrent and formed a sea of mud which crushed the houses
and drowned many of the inhabitants. From the train we
saw the wreckage of the little church, its roof smashed in, and
it helped to explain why in their country, where nature is so
beautiful but so unpredictable, there are many crucifixes. But
there is no smoke from Vesuvius. The top of the mountain
is now asymmetrical, its cone disfigured in the war. Perhaps
nature, recoiling from man's greater, more controllable, and
so more senseless violence, has in shame withdrawn her own
simple threat. A young man in the train said : 'Povero
Vesuvio ! Non può fumare più. Non ha il denaro.' A
putto in the opposite corner was reading a 'comic'. We
imagined that in this country of crimes of passion, landslides,
volcanoes, and blood so vital that it liquefies after a thousand
years, he must be filling his mind with superlative horrors.
On the station at Naples we bought one of these papers to see
how bad they were, but found them full of tales of lyrical
innocence. A boy with a flute plays so sweetly that he induces
an old curmudgeon to fling handfuls of gold to the poor. The
victim of a practical joke becomes tied to a danger notice and
so prevents a frightful accident, and it all ends in love and
flowers.

We also bought one of the more reputable English news-
papers, and the horror which we expected to feel at the
Corriere dei Piccoli now overwhelmed us. There was death
on every page, not the comparatively innocuous death we
might find plentifully in an Italian newspaper, the knifing of
a faithless lover, but the death of the soul. There are columns

AMALFI   31

in praise of Freud, surely the dreariest and most squalid of apostles ; there are letters from earnest provincial atheists ; there are reviews by young men of such extreme recondite erudition that it all seems gibberish to our half-educated minds, and the only books praised are those which describe entrails on an operating table, and sadism and stinking sanitation in a prison. They know every obscene autumnal fungus on the tree of human culture, which the bright hot sun of a new spring will shrivel, but are unaware of the tree itself. It seems to be the journal of a cultural suicide-club. It convinced us of the need, before we returned to our country where the old gods have died, to find new ones, or to discover the old ones to protect us, or to clothe ourselves in the humanity of Italy. This at least we can do. We cannot bring back, like our eighteenth-century antecedents, fine paintings and the designs of palaces to civilize our land, but we can bring back our lost humanity.

We only stayed in Naples for two days, to see the museum, though that really requires two months. We felt that in this wild city the Story might have taken on extravagant and morbid variations which would confirm in the Irish boy's mind the unfortunate impression made by the Manna of S. Andrew. On the way to the museum we risked a visit to the cathedral, though knowing that there was preserved the passionate dried blood of S. Januarius which, 1600 years after his martyrdom, pulses annually into life, not unlike that of Tennyson's hero, whose dust 'would start and tremble under her feet, and blossom in purple and red'. We looked through the grille of gilded bronze into the elaborate baroque chapel, where the blood is preserved in a bust of the saint, but did not feel the presence of any sympathetic noumenon. There is a fair amount for the sightseer in the cathedral, notably the renascence chapel in the crypt, but what delighted us most was a small boy who took a flying leap at the holy water stoup and hung on with one hand while he dipped in the other.

In a gallery to the right as we entered the museum, the statues of Harmodius and Aristogeiton greeted us like a shout — a shout so encouraging and alive that it dispelled as a wind from Greece the gloom of pointed arches and dried blood. The Irish boy declared at Paestum that he could not accept a story in which this splendid vigour was out of place. This is not to say that he contemplated becoming a muscular Christian, which he knows is a contradiction in terms. To develop the muscles beyond a certain point is to try to escape the demands of the spirit. The Greek development of the body was proportionate and in its beauty an expression of the spirit, of man reflecting the Perfect Drawing, unfallen, close to the gates of Paradise. The last thing the muscular Christian wants is to be beautiful. Harmodius and Aristogeiton are not muscular, nor are any of the Greek and Hellenistic statues we saw, except a few oppressive images of Heracles. Their muscles are in proportion to their bodies, kept within the lines of grace and beauty, and their spirits are aflame to destroy the Tyrant. Muscle developed beyond this proportion is a growth that blocks the movement of the spirit, and inevitably ends in fat.

It may seem perverse to go to this enormous house of treasures and merely mention these statues, but for the most part we only gave our attention to those things which relate to the Irish boy's search. He had in his mind the Zeus of Paestum, which later gave place to the Apollo of Veii, and now he put beside this image that of the Tyrannicides. They express something in his nature which he is prepared to have redeemed, but not destroyed.

We did not, of course, ignore everything else in the museum — the lovely Greek statues, the succession of rooms lined with wall-paintings from Pompeii, which are curiously modern in feeling and might have been painted by early French impressionists. There is a sculptured panel which attracted us, not so much aesthetically as for its strong sug-

gestion of symbolism. Mithras is sacrificing a bull. Is the
bull the symbol of the innocent life on this earth ? It is not
predatory. It lives on grass. It does not kill unless infuriated.
It lives peacefully according to its nature and the laws
of the Creative Nóos. But here it is attacked by a dog, a
scorpion, and a snake ; an animal that hunts for pleasure,
a deathly insect, and the reptile enemy of mankind. Does
this express a dim apprehension of the eternal sacrifice of
Christ ?

In the trolley-bus, going back to the hotel, again we met
the past of Italy in the present. Opposite us were Paquio
Proculo and his wife, whom half an hour earlier we had seen
in a Pompeiian wall-painting. They had only changed their
clothes — not an improvement.

On the railway station we met Hermes unredeemed, a
porter who arbitrarily took us in his charge. We asked for
the Rome train and he went to the booking-office to ask the
time and platform. He then went into a sort of information
bureau to ask again. When we pointed out that he had already
asked the booking-clerk, he replied : 'Perhaps he is a liar'.
He said this with such a complete absence of judgment that
for a moment we had a refreshing sense of moral freedom.
But we soon realized that it was like the sense of freedom
given by those between-the-war novels, written in a moral
vacuum, exhilarating at first, but now become the voice of
death.

The other seats in the railway carriage were taken by five
unacquainted people, who came in separately. Within a few
minutes of leaving Naples they were engaged in a discussion
of la vita moderna which had much to do with the design of
motor-cars. It lasted for nearly three hours, until we reached
Rome, where, after bouts of lively disagreement, they said
good-bye almost affectionately, as if they were old friends who
by accidental good fortune had travelled in the same train.
And so we ended this preliminary reconnaissance with a

further conviction of the goodness of humanity, without which all speculation about the nature of the unseen is only an intellectual indulgence.

In Rome we hoped to conduct our search with a more conscious sense of direction.

CHAPTER III

ROME: THE OLD GODS

In the vast atrium of the Termini station at Rome, the noumenon of the Irish boy, as all noumena must in the fullness of
time, achieved its phenomenon. So far, we must admit, he
had only been a part of our own mind, but now his physical
manifestation had come to meet us, dressed in grey flannel
and a yellow shirt, the colours of Hermes. He was excited
at being in Rome, and eager to begin, amongst all the riches
of its accumulated evidence, the search for his god.

He has agreed that the Supreme Nóos, groaning and
travailing to reveal himself to man, may first have given un-
certain intimations of his nature in Zeus, Apollo, and Pallas-
Athene, so we began our Roman search in the places where we
could find man's conception of them. The most primitive
are in the Etruscan museum in the Villa Giulia, which, incidentally, is rather hard to find. It is about half a mile along
the Via Flaminia, and then a few hundred yards to the right
up the Viale delle Belle Arti. Here we stood before the First
Face, that of the Apollo of Veii.

It is the face of the religion of the Paestum temples, and
there is something in our nature which responds to it with
delight. It is pure animal well-being. It has not been driven
from Paradise and so does not ask for redemption. It is in the
spiritual condition in which, in our times of perfect health,
we are satisfied to be. It has the rounded chin of someone
who is loved, yet it gives the impression of great strength. Its
braided hair, like a crown over its forehead, falls in ropes on
its splendid shoulders, and it shows carelessly the beauty of its
breast. But is it too savage to be part of that nóos which the

Irish boy will accept as his god ? The left eye has an almost
engaging humanity, but that strange protruding right eye
might have directed the flaying of Marsyas. It has a pride of
life which is alien to the temperament of people affected by
three centuries of puritanism.

Yet, if this is not the face of anyone driven from Paradise,
is it the face of man as he was first conceived in the mind of the
Creative Nóos ? Was man intended to have this complete
enjoyment of his physical being, and complete satisfaction in
the natural world, his home ? According to the Story, it was
through the development of intellectual and sensual curiosity
that he fell from innocence. The Apollo of Veii is not intellectual, and his sensuality would be physical and not inquisitive.
The Fall may have been necessary to develop our souls, but
when the soul has reached a certain stage of growth should it
not recover for its dwelling this perfect animal splendour ?
D. H. Lawrence thought that if he could return into the body
of the Apollo of Veii he would correct the imperfection of
his own drawing, but it was an impossible aim, and even if
he could have achieved it, the cost would have been the death
of his subtler faculties. The reunion must come about on a
different level.

The Irish boy admitted all this, but he would not repudiate
the Apollo of Veii as irrelevant to his search. On the contrary
he took it as the first contribution to the final image of his
god. If man fell morally on his exclusion from Eden, he also
fell physically, and if he is to recover his perfect being it must
include his body. The Incarnation was to restore us to
innocence, physical as well as of the soul, to restore to us 'the
innocent joy in all creation which is given to those who can
integrate their life with their faith'.[1] The Irish boy declared
that he intended to enjoy his body to its fullest extent, not in
mere beefy exercise, but in love and all good pleasures, and
his only restraint will be that he does no harm to others or to

[1] *Gothic Twilight*, Countess Nora Wydenbruck (Westhouse).

his body itself. He had been told that he 'should treat sex reverently'. He did not want to treat it reverently. He thought that people who did so would have the most ghastly prigs for children. He thought that sex at its best should have a ravishing beauty ; it would be like returning to live with the gods in the morning of the world. Even if it was not like that, he saw no reason why it should not be tremendous fun. Our bodies are the phenomena of noumena in the mind of the Creator, who saw that they were good, and we should gratefully enjoy them. It is ignoble and mean to reject his glorious gift by leading a deliberately deprived and emaciated life, which is much more a form of devil-worship than a full-blooded acceptance of the Apollo of Veii. He insisted that this part of his life had to be integrated with his faith. We agreed that it was a good aim, but thought that it might be difficult to achieve.

His conviction was strengthened by the Caere sarcophagus, the married couple seated at a banquet, again with that air of immense satisfaction. The Etruscans were renowned for their superstitions and enchantments, but their contacts must have been with noumena which increased their pleasure in the natural world. All those lively figures on the vases have the smiling lips of the Apollo and of the Zeus of Paestum, who also looked on the world and saw that it was good.

However, we did not look long at much else, as we are almost as careful to avoid sights as to seek them, not wishing to stun our minds with a confusion of images. Fortunately, in nearly every place in Rome where there is pre-Christian sculpture, there is also a garden where one may rest both the feet and the eyes. We walked out among the rose beds of the villa, and in the lovely loggia of Ammannati, above Vasari's nymphaeum, we discussed the rival claims of the flesh and the spirit. The Irish boy said :

'The world is good. If men had any sense they could all live in it with the greatest enjoyment. Nothing is perfect, not since the Fall, and there would be some sorrows and misfortune, but they would only be a fraction of experience. The Supreme Nóos created the good world and put us in it to enjoy ourselves. When Leo X said : "God gave us the Papacy, let us enjoy it", he was nearer wisdom than the ascetic who says : "God gave me a sound body, and the capacity for a healthy happy life. Let me starve it and make it ill, and so return to Him as soon as possible." God is our Father, but what father could tolerate a child who was always moaning how he loved him, and refusing every good gift he offered ? It is devil-worship. Our duty to God is to live happily in this marvellous world, following the natural laws, which are his own, and doing no harm to our brethren. Then if we have followed as far as possible the pattern of his intention for us in this world, he will see about rewarding us in the next. Our ills are of our own making. We spend fifteen hundred million pounds a year on weapons to kill our brethren, because we are devil-worshippers. We have not the courage to worship the good Nóos. We are cowards in the face of beauty. Just think what marvellous lives we could all have if that was spent on the good things of the world, on gardens, on glorious buildings, on everything lovely and living, on race-horses, if you like.'

It must be remembered that the Irish boy was young, at the beginning of his search, and that he had just been unconsciously worshipping the Apollo of Veii. Still, we did not entirely disagree with him.

*

Our next visit was to the museum in the Diocletian baths, called the Museo Nazionale. There is surely no place to which the hideous word national — a word like those others mentioned by Turgenev, that 'smell of blood' — could be more unsuitably given, for here the whole story of our civilization is contained within a few acres. Here, in these Roman baths, part of them turned by Michelangelo into a Christian church, are the loveliest fragments of Greek sculpture to be found in Italy. In the small cloister is that Aphrodite rising from the sea, carved five centuries before Christ, and breathing on us, if we have the senses to feel it, the pure strong air of the morning of the world. In this cloister is one of those untended gardens with their seldom-clipped box-hedges, the lilies of the bindweed and an occasional casual rose, which conform so much to the noumena of the place, and from it we can see a baroque belfry above Diocletian's wall. In the great cloister, that of the old Certosa, round the fountain where Michelangelo sat with Vittoria Colonna, are the cypresses he planted. Upstairs, as well as the finest mosaics, are others more crude which echo the play of Sicilian shepherds, and there are those delicate bas-reliefs brought from a Roman villa of the early Empire, and wall-paintings ; whole rooms painted, like those at Naples, almost in the style of the early French impressionists. So that if one could only spend a day in Rome, instead of rushing frantically round from S. Peter's to the Colosseum, to the Spanish Steps, it would be better to walk quietly across from the Termini station, about two hundred yards away, and to spend it here.

There could hardly be a more suitable place for the Irish boy, having been made aware in the Villa Giulia of the potentialities of animal well-being, to begin his search amongst more subtle influences — though he has by no means renounced the flesh, and he is, as it were, looking for a body which his god might inhabit. There are many statues here which could be divine images, but the finest is the Ephebe of Subiaco, the headless youth so perfect in its moulding and grace, in the texture and honey-colour of the marble, that we feel the living body, which it has made immortal, knew the sun and the sea-winds. It was drawn not by night, but in the clear morning light, which seems all-pervading in the evidence

of the Greek story, and which the Irish boy demands shall
surround his god. He knows that the Greeks had cruel
mysteries, but he is not groping after the evil, only the good
they have left. Later, when he came to the Christian story,
he found it also involved in atrocious evil, but he continued
his search.

This preliminary search for a body fit for his god may
sound like idolatry. Possibly, but we have no strong objection
to this kind of idolatry, having learned from people as far
apart as Wordsworth and D. H. Lawrence that it is better to
be a pagan suckled in a creed by no means entirely outworn,
than to find no meaning in what we see. Also we believe that
the noumena express themselves more truly in shapes than in
words, which are, like statues, only symbols that men have
made to describe them. Words can be used for an exact
statement of material fact, not of spiritual truth, which is best
conveyed by other symbols. To worship words is the more
sinister idolatry, and from it has resulted all the silliness and
cruel wickedness which has blackened the history of the
Church. The woman who teaches her baby to wave to the
Virgin, and the boy who puts his sprig of marjoram, whether
between the feet of Hermes or of Christ, harm no one. They
only fill their hearts with love.

And so, as the Irish boy is using his heart and his eyes to
find his god, the more images he sees, the wider is his field.
The Ephebe of Subiaco, most beautiful of all those in this
place, has no head, and so, though it stayed in our minds as a
symbol of physical perfection, it could not express divinity.
It was in the faces of the gods that we looked for their nature,
and when the Irish boy came to the Apollo of Tevere he
stopped as if he had found something that had led him a stage
onwards. A young man's god is his ideal of himself, himself
in Perfect Drawing, and at this stage of his search he believed
that the face of this statue satisfied his ideal. It is as much of
the morning as the Apollo of Veii, but the light is less harsh.

THE SECOND FACE.　The Apollo of Tevere

Museo delle Terme di Diocleziano

The eyes are reflective and the mouth is more gentle. It is not the Apollo who flayed Marsyas, but it might be the shepherd of Admetus. The forehead is wide and the thick hair covers his head like a cap. His strength and vitality are assured. It is not an intellectual head, but something far better, that of a man whose spirit is one with the flesh.

There are other statues here which drew our attention, as they gave those emanations of humanity which the Irish boy feels are the breath of life. Of these others the one that drew him most was that lightly veiled Aphrodite, perhaps of the fourth century, a fragment as full of grace as the Ephebe of Subiaco, and free of the tinge of sensuality — a sort of layer of fat under the skin — of the Hellenistic Aphrodite from Cyrene, at which he looked with rather clouded eyes.

We went out and sat on the low wall of the Certosa cloister. The heads of two enormous stone oxen loomed at us from the box-hedges, and under Michelangelo's cypresses some *putti* were dabbling in the fountain.

The Irish boy seemed preoccupied, and after sitting for some time in silence, he asked :

'If we are looking for an image which is the symbol of the Nóos, why couldn't it be the Aphrodite of Cyrene ?'

We replied that the Aphrodite was a deity with whom it was possible to have union in this world. She would most likely be necessary to his full life, but she could leave him, and he would be alone at the end. The nóos he was seeking was one that would live always in himself, so that he would recover that integrity and perfect harmony with the natural world and with the noumena beyond it which man had before the Fall, and which the animals still have on their level. It is to try to receive some impression of this that we are beginning our search amongst what evidence of the Greeks we can find in Rome, as they were nearer the gates of Paradise. In the Greek story, it is true, we find the noumenon which Plato calls the Uranian Aphrodite, which also is so powerful in the

D

Christian story, but that noumenon is equally a male principle, so even if you were to worship the Uranian Aphrodite, her image would have to have the almost masculine strength of the Electra standing with her arm on Orestes's shoulder in the Naples museum.

Although we were sitting in the cloister of the Certosa we did not want yet to enter the Christian story, not until we had received an impression of physical harmony with the created world. We had just accepted that a young man's god must be the image of his own nature made perfect, the rough sketch corrected and complete, living in himself. It is very easy to confuse his longing for his god with his longing for the Aphrodite of Cyrene, and for a time she may seem to satisfy it, but ultimately his god must appear to him as his own face in the mirror of perfection.

'Then,' said the Irish boy, 'shouldn't a girl's god be a woman?'

It was hard to answer this, but we did not profess to be able to answer all the thousand extremely difficult questions concerning the unseen, only possibly to be a rather diffident guide to the Irish boy in his intuitive search. We could only point out that in both the Greek and the Christian stories there was provision for a girl's need to worship a woman; also that the Uranian Aphrodite, so powerful in both, was, though predominantly male, also partly female; also that everyone, except the still primitive descendants of the cave man, had some modification from the other sex, and it was necessary that this ambiguity should also be found in the gods. The mistake was to imagine that the emotions aroused by the second-century Hellenistic Aphrodite of Cyrene (to our own mind pandemian) were the answer to the desire for what lay behind phenomena. Perhaps his greatest problem was to think together of the flesh and the spirit, and not to have them at war, a conflict which must end in the destruction of one of them, and we have agreed at Paestum that the body is good.

Before we left we went again to look at the Apollo of Tevere, and the Irish boy accepted that face as the symbol of the second stage of his search. The body was in harmony with the serene mind.

★

On the following day, averting our eyes from the immense glare of the Vittorio Emanuele memorial, we climbed the steps between the waving rows of oleanders to the Campidoglio, the piazza on the Capitolino Hill, where Marcus Aurelius, formerly thought to be Constantine, hails Rome from his horse. Facing each other across the piazza are the Conservatori and the Capitolino museums, and again with our selective laziness we only came to look, amongst all their treasures, at two or three statues. In the Capitolino museum we ignored the famous and disgusting dying Gaul, and the rows of emperors' heads. 'All great men are bad', and so have little beauty. Yet they not only do evil in their lives, but leave behind their horrible statues to disfigure the streets of our cities. If the streets of London could be cleared of politicians and generals, and filled with Greek gods and painted images of the blessed saints, what lightness of heart they might shed on us.

But even ignoring the emperors' heads there are few statues here that bring the sea-winds from Greece, that give us Mr. Berenson's tingling in the finger-tips which, however, we do not attribute only to technique. Or if it is due to technique, this was not the mere invention of their brains. Their gods were in themselves and they could not help revealing them in the Ephebe of Subiaco and the Aphrodite rising from the sea. In the later statues, the Graeco-Roman copies, the spirit has evaporated and only the heavy flesh is left.

This was true, we felt, of the copy of the Aphrodite of Cnidus and the faun of Praxiteles, but not of his Eros and Psyche. If the Irish boy is to worship an Aphrodite that is not

Uranian it is here that he can find its perfect phenomenon, and he looked at it with his lips faintly parted. Here is expressed all the tender innocence of first love. The group of the naked boy and the half-naked girl is entirely free from sensuality, as when, a little later in the same day, we saw an Italian boy in a café lean forward and put his arms gently round the girl who was with him, and for a moment lay his cheek lightly against hers, and then turn and continue his lively conversation with his other companions. He was filled with the same spirit as Praxiteles when he made these figures. For him the girl was a 'strange seraphic piece of life'.[1]

It was by this statue that we first saw a man who was to haunt us rather in our travels. He was between forty and fifty years old, with a bleak, sad, intellectual face, steel-rimmed glasses, thin hair, and in spite of these things a boyish appearance which may have been due to his wearing shorts, though the boyish effect was modified by the extreme hairiness of his legs. He was wearing also a green linen jacket, from a pocket of which stuck out a copy of the New Statesman.

He murmured 'sentimental', half to himself and half to us, and, looking cross, turned away from the statue. He was evidently one of those still in the process of reacting against the affectation of generous or tender or human feelings, who find themselves unable to distinguish between the affectation of the feelings and their genuine expression, and so in a state of irritation dismiss the lot. We discovered later that he attributed all the motions of the noumena as due simply to the functioning of glands, and was unaware that the glands are directed by the noumena, though he had experienced this himself on the lowest level of sensual stimulus. Being of puritan stock, though an atheist, he could not rid himself of the desire for salvation, and, like a vast number of people to-day, thought that it could be found in 'culture', though he also believed that the only function of art was to provoke

[1] *Centuries of Meditation*, Thomas Traherne.

physical sensations, the tingling in the finger-tips. To allow
it a meaning would be superstitious. Before the Eros and
Psyche we remembered : 'The greatness of man even in his
lust, to have known how to extract from it a wonderful code,
and to have drawn from it a picture of benevolence'.[1] The
man with the *New Statesman* in his pocket believes that Freud
has shown that code to be nonsense. All he can do is to try
to feel the tingling.

Apparently he achieved this in some degree before Praxiteles' faun, perhaps because it is not completely human, not
even as much as the Apollo of Veii. The faun is the happy
human body devoid of a soul, which may be the ideal of the
Freudians. But the faun, too, is a myth.

We crossed to the other museum in the Palazzo Conservatori, one of the most delightful places in Rome in which to
spend some sunlit hours, more so even than the Certosa
cloisters, for from there can be seen the tops of the commercial
buildings. Here, in the Conservatori gardens there is no
sight or sound to disturb their tranquillity, only the quiet
splash of the fountains. If the sun is too hot we can sit under
the bay trees or the ilex, or go in again to look at the lovely
fragments from the morning of the world — the torso of
Hermes ; the Esquilino Aphrodite whose body is like a spring
flower ; the famous boy with his archaic head on a Hellenistic
body, who is taking a thorn from his foot, a slight but eternal
thing in human experience.

Time spent in this way may not much help the Irish boy
in his search, beyond strengthening in him that attitude to
our physical nature which is expressed by these figures ; but
it does give him a glimpse of the life led by his forebears of the
last century, those leisurely travellers from the British Isles,
who drove about a Rome where the dominant sound was the
splash of the fountains. Some of their names we find amongst
the cypresses of the Protestant cemetery, given a sanction

[1] *Pensées*, Pascal.

which otherwise they might lack, by the presence there of
Keats's body and Shelley's heart.

*

Continuing in the pagan world, we next went to the
Vatican museum, on this visit only to see the pre-Christian
statues.   But in these galleries there are few sea-winds from
Greece. The Roman sculpture and the Graeco-Roman copies,
much restored, at their best were very remote relatives of
the rising Aphrodite and the Ephebe of Subiaco.   Even the
much-admired Apollo Belvedere and Hadrian's favourite,
Antinous, have a slightly oily, expensive look about them.
In modern clothes they would not be noticeable in the
Ritz bar.

But in the far corner of Bramante's noble Court of the
Belvedere, where flowering shrubs, growing in great stone
vases, fill the air with sweet and heavy scent, there is an engaging and lovely Hermes. Nicholas Poussin told him that he
had the most perfect young male body in the world, so in
modesty he retired to this secluded niche ; but it did not save
him from a cruel ravishment. For in the last few years all
the male statues in the Vatican galleries have been mutilated
and fitted with white plaster fig-leaves, which have not even
been toned to the colour of the marble. On this Hermes,
whose jaunty hat was surely sufficient clothing, and whose
marble is of a beautiful honey-gold texture, the contrast is
grotesque. What can this innocent and integrated youth,
in whom soul and body are one, think of this joke, as it must
appear to him, which has turned him into an obscenity ?
Were the priests who ordered this angry at his closeness
to the gates of Paradise, from which themselves are driven
so far ?

The Irish boy was full of angry contempt, and as usual
when he had seen as much as he could digest, here rather more,

he led the way out of doors, and we sat under a pine tree on the terrace, looking across the gardens to Michelangelo's dome. He felt that what had been done to the Hermes was the Church's threat to himself. How could the authorities who ordered this, he asked, command respect when they did not show it to an antiquity greater than their own?

On coming to Rome we had intended to ignore the Christian story until we had made an excursion into the Graeco-Roman world, but here it had been disagreeably forced upon us, not in its purity but in its perversion. When at Amalfi we glanced at its outline, the Irish boy accepted it, at any rate as a working hypothesis. He admitted that the gods, beautiful and full of meaning as they were, needed redemption, but to mutilate them is not to redeem them. In this place, where they are the captives of the Church, he could see its real intention towards his physical life. He was inclined to accuse us of deceiving him in our presentation of the Story, and he went over it again.

Our bodies are the phenomena of noumena in the mind of the Creator, conceived by him in their desires and in every detail, beautiful, perfect, and good. The Hermes in the court of the Belvedere is as near as we can imagine to that perfect conception. Through an evil use of our intellect we impaired the integrity of our souls, and as a result our bodies too became flawed. Our whole aim is to recover that double perfection, and so that we might have the pattern, God re-created man in innocence, the Second Adam. All those mutilated statues deny the doctrine of the Incarnation. Their mutilation was an act of heresy, as Origen, who performed the same crime on himself, could never become a saint. Has some Vatican official the competence to improve or deface the image conceived in the mind of the Eternal Good?

We admitted that the Irish boy had come up against what might prove a major obstacle in his search, but we asked him to put it aside until we came to where we found its strongest evidence. We left the Vatican and went elsewhere to look for signs of redemption.

*

The riches of Italy are so vast that no book can mention more than a fraction of them, which is why it is allowable to go on writing Italian travel books. Every writer may see something new, or from a different angle. For the same reason it is allowable to ignore anything, however important, which may be outside one's mood. So, though still moving in pre-Christian Rome, we ignored its greatest evidence, the Forum. It is more a place for scholars than for those using only the heart and the eye ; though there are beautiful group-ings, the arch of Septimus Severus against a baroque dome, or a few columns against the Palatine hill. But to walk in this graveyard of temples, and be told which gods were worshipped in them, would not stimulate our imagination, perhaps because we feel that these Roman gods were more like the Apollo Belvedere, than of Tevere or of Veii.

The Colosseum is not entirely a ruin, and it is relevant to our search. It is where the gods of Paestum, in their obese and brutal old age, met the new non-violent faith and were de-feated and redeemed. It is not a beautiful place today. If it still had its marble covering, or the shrubs sprouting from its walls as in eighteenth-century prints, it might be picturesque, but it is too big. It is out of scale with human life. Here the Irish boy had his first intimation of that menace which later appalled him, and which he thought was entirely of the modern world, a 'civilization' out of scale with humanity. Not only the building itself, but all that happened in it was out of the human scale, except one incident which closed its hideous record.

Like Versailles, another expression of megalomania, it was cursed from the beginning. Its marble was taken from Nero's palace, and later stripped by renascence popes. Here, for four centuries, the fights, at first between two gladiators, became more wholesale to satisfy the mounting blood lust of the mob. Under Augustus 10,000 gladiators were used in only eight fights. Women and children were thrown naked to the beasts. Prisoners from all over the known world were made to kill each other. Here we first meet something which again had seemed to belong exclusively to the modern world, those terrible rows of noughts behind a figure, which are the only gauge of human anguish.

So violent was the passion of the Romans to watch death agonies, that even the decrees of the Christian emperors could not stop the shows. Before that could happen the old gods, the Apollo of Veii, that smiling mouth dripping with blood, had to be redeemed, and by a willing Christian sacrifice.

The Irish boy had not accepted that the death of Christ was a sacrifice demanded by the savage nostrils of the Jewish tribal god, but only as an inevitable result of the Incarnation, of the perfect coming into contact with the imperfect, which cannot endure it. It was not desired by the Supreme Nóos, the true Father of Heaven, any more than a man who sees his son going into battle wishes him to be killed.

The war in Heaven is not over. The sacrifice of the monk Telemachus, who ended the murderous shows, was not pleasing to God. His wounds and death were not pleasing — to that extent the devil had won. His courage and love were pleasing, and outshone the evil of his death. He could not bear the thought of this mass butchery, and he came to Rome to try to stop it. But if the edicts of the emperors were powerless, it was unlikely that the efforts of a provincial monk would be effective. So, failing other means, he entered the arena and tried to separate the gladiators with his hands, and was killed. This death he accepted of his own will, unlike all those other victims who had death forced upon them. At the sight of this willing sacrifice, there awoke in the people, brutalized through four centuries of stimulated blood lust, that spark of humanity without which we cannot live. They recoiled in shame and the shows ended for ever.

For centuries afterwards the Colosseum was avoided as a place of horror. It was used as a quarry. At one time it was inhabited by wolves. It was not until thirteen centuries later that Benedict XIV, seeing it had not only been a place of great evil, but a place where that evil was overcome by good, dedicated it to the Passion of Christ.

So in the Colosseum we are in the meeting-place between the old gods and the new, the old gods become bestial and trying to stamp out the new life, but finally defeated and redeemed, not by their mutilation, but by the willing sacrifice of the innocent, through which their own innocence was restored. For the old gods, as we have realized, are largely ourselves. It is the restoration of our innocence which we require, not our mutilation.

When we left the Colosseum the Irish boy was ready to explore further into the Christian story.

CHAPTER IV

THE INNOCENT CHURCHES

WE took a 60 bus from the Piazza Barberini to S. Agnese fuori le Mura, a mile or so beyond the Porta Pia, along the Via Nomentana. Here is another meeting-place between the old gods and the new, and here finally we passed right into the Christian story.

S. Agnese was a beautiful child, barely thirteen years old. The son of the Prefect of Rome saw her coming from school, and wanted to marry her, but she snubbed him, saying, like S. Catherine a thousand years later, that she was already the bride of Christ. The youth became ill, and the doctor told the prefect that he 'languished of a carnal passion'. S. Agnese was given the choice of accepting the prefect's son, or of being sent to the brothel. She chose the latter, knowing that she would be protected. There she was surrounded with a white light so that no one dared approach her, and finally she was dispatched with a sword.

This kind of martyrdom was less agreeable to the Irish boy than that of S. Telemachus. It was against, while the other was for, humanity. The idea of young people refusing a human lover — and at the beginning the prefect's son had a very proper and touching desire for her — in favour of a spiritual one, is repugnant to him. He feels that the noumena should direct and protect our loves on this earth, not compete in them. And was it very saintly of her, when he honourably offered her marriage, to retort : 'Go from me, thou fardel of sin' ? [1]

After her death she was party to another spiritual marriage.

[1] *The Golden Legend.*

51

A priest, very much tempted of the flesh, was told by the pope to put an emerald ring on the finger of her statue. The hand closed on it and thereafter he was free of his lust.

If all this is true, it would seem that S. Agnese had only escaped the first temptation to plunge straight into the third ; but the account is coloured by medieval imagination, and the actual martyrdom may have been a clear and classic tragedy. We know that it happened in about A.D. 250 under the persecutions of the Emperor Decius.

In the church, where she is buried under the altar, are some fine Corinthian columns, and a seventh-century mosaic, but the rest has suffered from one of those restorations which baffle us everywhere in Rome. They are like the Counter-Reformation which effected them, covering the serene strength of the undivided church with a fictitious exuberance of life, which is neither that of the pagan body nor of the Christian soul. Here on the feast of S. Agnese, lambs decked out with garlands of flowers are offered on the altar, and again the old religion meets the new, for this must be a survival from the days when the wreathed beasts were led to sacrifice. But the Christian modification is effected. The lambs are not killed ; only their wool is taken to be woven into the *pallia* which the pope sends to newly appointed archbishops.

We gave our attention to the mosaic in the apse, as it was the first we saw of those which are found in nearly all the early Roman churches. They are important in the Irish boy's search, as they are almost the first expression in art of the Christian noumena. In this one S. Agnese is arrayed like a Byzantine empress, supported by Honorius and another pope, the donors. The Irish boy asked if these were the rewards for which the early Christians suffered martyrdom. How is it that this art, which evolved after a few hundred years of Christianity, is so inferior to that which it should have redeemed, the mosaics in the Diocletian museum, and those which we saw half an hour later, in S. Costanza down the lane ? Are not these mammoth saints which stare at us from the barbaric splendour of their tribunes, glittering with gold and magnificence of colour, more *décor* than art ? Is there any meaning in their expressionless faces, which all seem to be related to Paquio Proculo, but without his intelligence ? They are certainly magnificent *décor*, and when a whole church is done with them, as at S. Mark's in Venice, their noumena are potent, they symbolize with a spirit, and we are transported into another atmosphere, as powerfully as by the temples at Paestum.

But even with the mosaics we were a little ahead of our period, which is that of S. Agnese herself, and we had to remember that she who still lived in the age of classic art might have been as repelled by this Byzantine idea of her heavenly reward, made five centuries later, as was the Irish boy.

A lively and entertaining priest asked us if we would like to see the catacomb. If the blood of the martyrs was the seed of the Church it was only right that we should see where it had been sown, deep in the earth, to germinate there until, with Constantine, it could send up its green shoots and blossom in the light. All the same, we did not want to spend hours groping in underground tunnels, and as the catacomb here is small and can be seen in ten minutes, we were glad of the opportunity to perform this act of piety with such brief discomfort. Holding lighted tapers, we went through the honeycombs of tunnels, with their shelves holding handfuls of dust, the buried seed, all that is left of physical agony. On one shelf was a small skull, and the priest with ironical Catholic pessimism said : 'Miss Universe'. At the end of our cramped and gloomy trek, peering in the dim light of the tapers, with an air of malicious amusement he switched on the electric light with which the whole place was fitted.

At the door of S. Costanza, a hundred yards away, he made us turn to look at a 'typical Roman scene' ; and it might have been so a century ago, with the church, the cypresses, and the orchard sloping away down the hill-side.

Costanza, only a courtesy saint, was the daughter of the Emperor Constantine, and was cured of leprosy by a vision of S. Agnese, in gratitude for which she founded the church we have just seen. All the same she must have died young, as her father built for her this round mausoleum. In the seventeenth century the mosaics in the dome were destroyed in a 'restoration' which was one of the worst minor vandalisms Rome has known. Those that remain in the circular side aisle show us what we have lost — delicate and lovely and gay, with *putti* and vine leaves, celebrating the vintage harvest. They are in the transition between Christian and pagan art. In them the pagan gods are redeemed, not yet mutilated or driven out. They faced the Irish boy with a problem, which, in different forms, he repeatedly met in his search.

'How is it,' he asked, 'that four centuries of Christianity, which brought the spirit into the material world, could change its expression from this clear loveliness, to the crude mosaics of the apse?' The spirit descended into matter to illuminate it, he said. Somewhere he had read that classical art was characterized by 'light on' and Christian by 'light through'. To everyone who is aware of the noumena behind phenomena, the natural world is infinitely more beautiful. 'The earth, and every common sight . . . did seem apparelled in celestial light.' [1] The man who is aware of the Christian noumena can write : 'The green trees when first I saw them through one of the gates, transported and ravished me ; . . . young men (were) glittering and sparkling angels, and maids strange seraphic pieces of life and beauty ! Boys and girls, tumbling in the street and playing, were moving jewels.' [2] This was how the redeemed should see life, the Irish boy protested, but here the *putti*, the tumbling jewels, are on the pagan ceiling, and the barbaric empress, no seraphic piece of life, in the Christian apse.

[1] 'Intimations of Immortality', Wordsworth.
[2] *Centuries of Meditation*, Thomas Traherne.

We suggested as a parallel that four centuries after Benvenuto Cellini, people can accept as sculpture preposterous distortions, or bits of wire and concrete.

'But those are just a hoax,' said the Irish boy, 'or else sheer degeneracy. The people who made these mosaics in the apse were serious, and doing the best they could. They have a crude magnificence, but there are no noumena behind them. They're just *décor.*'

Perhaps an explanation was that at that time the pagan culture had died. There is a theory that human civilization moves in cycles of two thousand years, each in some relation to a sign of the zodiac. The classical culture was under the Ram. Ares in Greece was the god of virtue, and only in the decadence became the god of war. The Christian period, which now in its rigid ecclesiastical forms seems to be weakening, was under the Fish, episcopus, the name given to bishops. The Christian noumena had come to inspire a new belief, not to revive the dying.

'But we agreed,' protested the Irish boy, 'that the old gods are redeemed, not dead.'

We explained that the early Christians believed that they were dead. We cannot always be consistent. Sometimes two good things may appear to us irreconcilable — the serenity of the Apollo of Tevere and the serene faith of the saints of the catacombs. We shall not give up either, believing that all things comely are reconciled in the mind of the Supreme Nóos. If we were entirely consistent, we should be like Tennyson with the daisy. We would understand God and our brains would burst. Besides, *le dieu défini est le dieu fini,* that is, if he is defined in the limited mind of man.

At this stage of our search we had better pigeon-hole the old gods in our minds, taking them out occasionally for reference. Perhaps in Christianity there was always a tendency to regard phenomena, not as the expression of noumena, but as divorced from them, particularly in Protestantism which prefers to ignore the Incarnation. We were not sure that the Irish boy had not a tendency towards pantheism, which of the two errors we much prefer. But we reminded him that he was not seeking his god through the use of his intellect, which was entirely inadequate to the purpose. If he were to attempt this method, he would have to spend his life in a university library, bewildered by mountains of theological argument, the impotent in full pursuit of the incomprehensible. For even the doctors of theology, who in our eyes are great and learned men, in the eyes of the Supreme Nóos may only be presumptuous ants.

All we can do is to go to those places where the noumena may speak to us, either to our hearts — through the emanations from ancient stones — or more explicitly to our eyes, in images and fine paintings and buildings. So we went to S. Giorgio in Velabro, where they speak to the heart.

It is in the old market-place of the Greek quarter, between the Palatine and the Tiber, next to the Arch of the Goldsmiths. To enter the church one has to ring the bell of the adjoining monastery and ask permission, which is always given.

Though this church has been restored, it is to its primitive simplicity, with mica instead of glass in the stone-barred windows. All is soft and grey, and the church is a bride as yet unadorned. Its sixteen columns, as at S. Agnese, have been taken from some pagan building, but here collected from odd sources, and are of different orders, placed directly on the floor without bases. In spite of these columns the atmosphere is purely Christian. The greyness is only relieved by the faded colours of the frescoes in the apse. The walls are not parallel, and the wooden ceiling is not quite a rectangle. Through an open doorway on the south, the sunlight filtered down to a little stream which trickles through ferns and ancient stones.

S. Giorgio was founded in the fourth century, but much that gives the feeling of antiquity is later — the canopy over the altar with its rows of small columns, and the mosaics of the Cosmati, those brothers who, in the twelfth century, left their mark on the churches of Rome, in pulpits and ambones and the circular designs in pavements. Yet here people worshipped who had lived under persecution, and here the mass must have been celebrated while the gladiators were still fighting in the Colosseum, half a mile away, before the martyrdom of Telemachus. It is easy to feel the noumena in this place, where for so long those who had combined perfect gentleness with perfect courage, at last emerged from underground, from those dreadful catacombs where the seed had grown strong roots, to sing their praises in the light of day, like a plant opening its leaves in the sun. For nearly all their hymns were to the light :

> Hail gladdening light of his pure glory poured, who
>   is the immortal Father . . .

> O Blest Creator of the light,
> Who mak'st the day with radiance bright,
> And o'er the forming world didst call
> The light from chaos first of all.

> Rank on rank the host of heaven spreads its vanguard
>   on the way, as the Light of Light descendeth . . .

All these hymns of the fourth, fifth, and sixth centuries echo in this church where they must have been sung when they were first composed, and they are all simple and innocent statements like the building itself. In these early centuries the Irish boy found the Christian story easy to accept, for, after all, it was only light that he was seeking ; and the serene light in which those people lived, like that described in *Marius* during the minor peace of the Church, seemed to him to have retained something of the light which shone from the head of the Apollo of Tevere. The innocent confidence of those early hymns, their freedom from strained emotion, is in itself evidence that they were written by people in whom the gods

E

of proportion had not yet died. They are like the transitional mosaics in S. Costanza, but they are also a slight reconciliation of the oppositions we felt in that place.

S. George is the patron of England, and his head is buried under the altar. Perhaps appropriately this church expresses, more than any other in Rome, that ideal of primitive Catholicism to which the Anglican Church officially appeals. Possibly the beauty of S. Giorgio is that of a leaf from which the green flesh has withered ; in this, too, we may later find a parallel with Anglicanism. But the noumena have not fled ; they are only sleeping, waiting to be aroused by one of those incantations to the light. Though here the antiquity and the sense of civilization are so much greater, the feeling is something like that we have in an old English country church, as yet spared restoration.

For antiquity is comparative. On the way from S. Giorgio to its younger sister, S. Maria in Cosmedin, only a short distance, we see across the road the temple of Fortune, built about five hundred years before Christ, and the famous little round temple called the temple of Vesta, but really that of the Goddess of the Dawn ; so here the light was worshipped nine centuries before those ancient hymns were sung in S. Giorgio. In our sight all these centuries are telescoped, and but an evening gone.

Rome is built on Rome, which is why the uncovered Forum is twenty feet lower than the rest of the city. The columns of S. Maria in Cosmedin are also from a pagan temple, probably the temple of Ceres over which it is built. Although this church is a little later than S. Giorgio, in the crypt under the high altar is a tiny chapel which was in use in A.D. 200, and in it are the bones of many martyrs, and those who worshipped here risked being thrown to the lions with every hymn they sang.

In the church above are many beautiful things, an eighteenth-century mosaic inscribed θεοτόκῳ ἀεὶ παρθένῳ ; the cosmata pavements ; the delicate gold mosaics on the ambones ; the twisted candelabra ; the canopy over the altar, and the enclosed marble choir, where today, instead of the communicants separating themselves from the catechumens, any Christians take refuge from the tourists. As the bell rang and the priest with his acolytes entered from the sacristy, a group of about twenty of these dazed and bewildered people, who were probably seeing all Rome in three days, entered with their guide, who rattled out the main points of interest, while the priest had to push his way through them to reach the altar. We imagined this to be an isolated incident, but it turned out to be an omen of things to come.

S. Maria in Cosmedin has undergone a process similar to that 'crystallization' which Stendhal describes as part of the process of love. First we have the temple of Ceres, the mother of the fruitful earth and of our bodies. Then came that tiny chapel where our souls began to grow, where the seed was planted which later flowered in the church above. Then appeared the mosaic in which the mother of our bodies has become the Mother of our souls, and finally, in that post-renascence chapel of the Blessed Sacrament, the corn of Ceres has become the Body of Christ.

The intimations we received from these early churches were much the same, and they were perhaps strongest in the three we had now visited ; but we also were tourists, and though we wished to avoid the condition of those who, with numbed eyes, blocked the passage of the priest to the altar, we did not confine ourselves exclusively to those places and things which were likely to mark stages in the Irish boy's understanding. If our meals consisted only of food which could be counted on as pure nourishment, our digestive organs would suffer.

We remained, however, for a few days in the ethos of the early Church. Perhaps some reader who finds himself in Rome may like to follow in the steps of our pilgrimage, and for his benefit we may act occasionally as a guide-book.

There is a garland of these early churches on and around the Coelian hill. When we walk up from S. Maria in Cosmedin the first of them at the foot of the hill is S. Gregorio Magno, but along the Valle delle Camene, where one may rest under the trees, past the Baths of Caracalla, is S. Nereo e Achilleo, and a little farther on S. Cesareo. Both echo the hymns to the light, but in the former the atmosphere is more potent, as a fifteenth-century cardinal, with a respect for existing architecture altogether extraordinary in a renascence Roman, prayed posterity that it might always retain its original state. Here, and at S. Cesareo, a martyr who under Diocletian was flung into the sea in a sack, are some of the finest works of the Cosmati in pavements and pulpits. In this neighbourhood is the church of S. Giovanni in Olio, S. John in Oil, commemorating an attempt to martyr this saint by boiling him. Next door to S. Cesareo, amongst trees and lawns, is the pavilion of Cardinal Bessarione, very like a modern house, where it would be delightful to live.

However, it was at S. Gregorio Magno that we began our walk over the Coelian hill. The great flight of steps, the cypresses, the renascence façade to the atrium, again, as when we looked back at S. Agnese, recall vividly the Roman scene as it must have appeared to our travelling countrymen of the last century, those who now lie under the cypresses near the Pyramid of Cestius.

S. Gregorio Magno, Pope Gregory I, was born and lived on the site of this church. His mother is buried in one of the trinity of chapels in the grass enclosure at the side. The church has been much 'done over', and, whenever we saw it, was filled with lilies and gold chairs for a wedding, but the cosmata pavement remains, particularly rich in colour and design. The two side chapels might be Louis XV *salons*, but off the one on the right is S. Gregory's cell, and in it is his marble chair, much worn, but with the low relief carving on the back still unspoiled. Also, in one of the trinity of chapels, is

a large marble table where every day he waited on twelve
poor men whom he brought in from the highways and hedges.
In those days bishops lived completely in the Story, and in
actions like this the symbol and the truth behind it were fused
together. S. Gregory, too, recalls the other story, for when
he saw the English boys in the market-place, like the Greek
soldier who would spare the life of a beautiful youth in battle,
he said they were too angelic to be damned, and sent S.
Augustine to save them. As he also was a musician, we
touched his chair with reverence, feeling that virtue must
remain in the place where lived this great and good man.

Through a door on the other side of the church we could
see into a garden with vines and fruit-trees, where a monk
was digging vegetables. On this still summer afternoon we
thought we had a glimpse of the perfect life, close to nature,
labouring amongst the fruits of the earth, while a few yards
away the fruits of the earth had become the Body of Christ.

A steep, high-banked lane leads from S. Gregorio up to
SS. Giovanni e Paolo, not the John and Paul of the New
Testament, but two court officials in the reign of Julian, who
were executed in their own house, which is under the church
where they are buried. This church too has been 'done over',
but from it we went down into the house where the two
martyrs lived, the only complete Roman private dwelling in
existence. As we went through these small windowless
rooms, we wondered at the tales of the luxury of Imperial
Rome. They look as if, under the best conditions, they must
always have been damp and airless ; while on the Palatine,
the House of Livia, if only it had a pond, would seem more
suited to a sea-lion than a dowager empress. So this house is
more a place for the antiquary than for the pilgrim or the
artist, as little is known of the two saints, and the wall-
paintings are nothing to those we saw at Naples. Yet we
received something from this place, as we realized at the end
of our walk.

A few hundred yards beyond SS. Giovanni e Paolo, we came to a gateway, and to a further reminder of those rows of noughts which are the sum of human suffering, but here redeemed. Over the gateway of an old convent is a cosmata mosaic, in which Christ stands between a black and a white slave. This was the convent of the Trinitarians, an order founded in the twelfth century for the ransom of prisoners. Through their labours 900,000 returned to freedom. During our pilgrimage, we were subject to phases of prejudice against monks, but if an assessment could be made of their good and ill contributions to humanity, we feel that the balance, ignored by the Whig histories which coloured our youthful minds, would be on the credit side. After Henry VIII, for the first time in our history the poor became a problem for legislation, and it is hard to see that the 'nobles' who seized the Church lands were more beneficial to the country than the abbots. In our own time it is an English monk who tried to stand between the black men and the white in Africa, and so this gateway influenced the Irish boy.

Along to the right is S. Maria in Domnica, or Navicella, so called because of the fountain in the form of a boat which stands before it. The church, originally built in the fourth century, has twice been restored, but it is simply impressive, with ninth-century mosaics. Again we asked ourselves whether these striking designs and colours convey much meaning, any intimation too elusive to be contained in an intellectual statement. Do these rows of Paquio Proculos with their haloes, their white robes and the lilies sprouting at their feet, attempt to convey the noumena of the Holy Apostles, or are they merely a decorative statement of their existence ?

Across the road S. Stephano Rotondo is said to be one of the most interesting early churches in Rome, but there is little hope of seeing it, as it is undergoing restorations which will last ten years. It contains hideous paintings of the torments of the damned, the medieval equivalent of 'X' films.

THE INNOCENT CHURCHES 63

Down the hill is S. Clemente, where Rome has doubly built itself on Rome. S. Clemente is not only built above an original lower basilica, but below that is the house of S. Clement himself, now a damp and rather frightening dungeon, including a sinister cave of Mithras. But here lived the friend of S. Paul, the friend and successor of S. Peter, so down below these superimposed basilicas we came to the very fountain and origin of the Roman Church.

In the church itself, on the right as we enter, is a chapel painted by Masolino. The marble enclosed choir with its ambones of the sixth century was brought up to the 'new' basilica from the old, and from it, too, must have risen the early hymns to the light. Here the mosaics in the apse are more purely decorative, scrolls of the vine with few figures, more in proportion to the church than those black-fringed faces which we see elsewhere. At this stage, feeling that our eyes might become numb and our brains confused with visions, we went to rest in the cloister with its cobblestones and weeds, its trickling fountain, its antique columns and sun-baked tiles, and a few pot-plants.

The Irish boy sat against one of the columns; he appeared reflective but contented. He felt that such evidence of the early Church as he had seen had helped him in his search. What he found disagreeable in the story of S. Agnese he attributed to medieval discoloration. The early Christian light does not seem to him to dispel the Greek sunlight but to include it as the pagan columns are included in S. Giorgio. He does not expect to escape cruelty and suffering, but they must be acknowledged as the inflictions of the devil. He cannot worship a god who mutilates his own creation.

We walked from S. Clemente, down past the Colosseum to SS. Cosma e Damiano, the last of what the Irish boy called 'the innocent churches' of our pilgrimage. Here Vespasian's temple of Peace was burnt in the second century. It was restored and turned into a church in the sixth, the adjoining temple being used as a vestibule. In the seventeenth century, the level of Rome rising with the dust of ruins, it was so far underground that a Barberini pope had a new floor built half-way up the church. The mosaics, perhaps the most splendidly sombre and barbaric in Rome, are thus even more out of proportion to the church than they were originally, and the forbidding face of Christ looms above us, more in threat than in love. It was certainly not the Third Face for which the Irish boy had begun to look, the Face of the complete and perfect Nóos which he would accept for his god.

One reason why we visited these churches was because of their names : Clement, John and Paul, Cosmas, and Damian. These five names are recited daily throughout the world in the most sacred of Christian prayers, the Canon of the Mass, and have been through all the centuries since their death. We may have heard them in far countries, but when they are repeated here, above the very houses where these men lived, they take on a new meaning. For they were not inserted in the Canon as myths of remote antiquity, but with grief and love, as today the names might be remembered of friends who had been butchered in Hitler's Germany or in Hungary. So, standing above the house of SS. Cosma e Domiano we become more aware of the reality of our place in history.

CHAPTER V

S. MARIA MAGGIORE, MOSES
AND S. CROCE

S. MARIA MAGGIORE is not an 'innocent' church, in the way those we saw in the last chapter are innocent. It is of the same or of an even earlier period, but in its structure it is without poetry, or at any rate the lyrical poetry of S. Giorgio. It is grand and solidly planted on this earth. It is perhaps the most impressive and has the most dignity of all the churches in Rome. It does not attempt to impress by mere size, but by proportion, and by the rows of noble columns which lead like an avenue to the rich focal point of the altar and the tribune. It was most likely a basilica, a hall of justice of pagan Rome, before Pope Liberius in A.D. 359 added an apse and made it a Christian church. In the *confessio*, that kind of well before the high altar, Pio Nono in marble adores a piece of the true manger from Bethlehem.

Though here we found what most satisfies our hearts and minds, classical proportion Christianized, the two Stories perfectly united, we also, for the first time since leaving Paestum, were made aware of another story. We came here to see the mosaics above the rows of Roman columns. They are possibly of the second and third centuries. They have not the gaiety of those in S. Costanza — there are no vine leaves and tumbling jewels — but they show more power of expression than the black-fringed faces on the Coelian hill. They are not rigid giant dolls, but figures able to move. They are, however, figures from the Old Testament, that third story which we are told is the necessary foundation of the Christian story, and often, particularly in Protestant countries, so involved in it that the authority of the two is regarded as equal. The Irish boy looked at the mosaics through a pair of opera glasses, but when we left the church he said : 'I loathe the Old Testament.'

The noumena which we hoped were directing our search had suddenly concentrated our attention on the Hebrew story, and unconsciously obeying them, we turned our steps away from S. Prassede, where we had intended to see various relics — the column of the scourging and S. Pius X's enormous shoes ; and we walked away down the hill, and up the steps under the archway to S. Pietro in Vincolo, the home of Michelangelo's 'Moses'. This statue, enormous as it is, was intended as only part of the mammoth tomb of Julius II, the war-mongering adventurer whose life is briefly satirized in Erasmus's dialogue 'Julius Exclusus', which describes this pontiff's arrival at the gate of Heaven and his interview with S. Peter.

With this statue, Michelangelo, who could make men like gods, has become bogged down in the Old Testament, and has only produced pomposity. The Irish boy finds it entirely repulsive, the coarse nose, the gross beard, the thick-veined hands, and the inexplicable horns ; or are they an indication that the Old Testament is woven throughout with devil worship ?

Standing before this 'Moses', the Irish boy heatedly re-pudiated that book, of which, though he had heard it read since childhood, he seemed only in the last hour to have become fully aware. He could accept many of its cautionary tales, such as those of the Golden Calf and the Tower of Babel. They are full of meaning for us today. He could accept the first Chapter of Genesis, which so upset the nineteenth-century scientists. It is a very clear symbolic statement of the condi-tion in which we find ourselves, fallen from innocent intuitive life, which makes necessary redemption by the Second Adam. His objection is moral, not scientific. He realizes now that

as he sat in church as a boy, listening to those lessons about
savage kings, going round self-righteously slaughtering every
foreigner they could lay hands on, smashing all the temples
and the glorious statues — they would have smashed the
temples at Paestum, the Ephebe of Subiaco, and Aphrodite
rising from the sea — that as he listened to those dreary
denouncing prophets, who doubtless had beards like this
hideous statue, his inexpressible boredom was due to a profound instinctive moral repudiation. It was the boredom we
feel when we are asked to give respectful attention to a lie,
the lie that God the Father could behave like a vicious and
jealous woman.

'Don't the clergymen who read this stuff,' he asked, 'realize
that people leave the Church not because it is incompatible
with their scientific knowledge, such as it is, but with their
moral understanding ?'

God is simply the sum of all good, he went on, and so we
worship him. But how can we worship, for example, a god
who played that sadistic trick on Abraham ? If we knew a
man who had done such a thing to a friend, had caused him
through anticipation half the anguish of murdering his son,
we should think him utterly vile. We cannot worship what
is lower than ourselves, and the noumenon which put that
intention into the mind of Abraham could not have been
from the sum of Good, but from the sum of Evil, which is the
devil.

The Pope begged Henry VIII not to have the Bible translated into English, not because, as Protestants pretend, he was
afraid of its truth, but because he knew that the people would
be unable to distinguish between those barbaric tales and
Christian truth ; and that, as happened, they might justify a
Cromwell in the massacre of Drogheda and the destruction
of centuries of art in the churches ; and in our own time, the
endorsement by Anglican bishops of the holocausts of Dresden
and Hiroshima, those rows of noughts. For half the Old

Testament can only corrupt those who believe it is the Word of God. It is responsible for most of the evils of the modern world, excessive nationalism, wars that were righteous instead of the wicked pastimes of princes, and that array of 'great men', who, as Lord Acton declared, are usually bad. All the puritan references, all the justification for their barbarism, comes from the Old Testament, from which they even chose the names of their children. Cromwell, the Covenanters, and the whole murderous brood of the 'righteous' have no relation to Christianity. If the noumenon which inspired their devilries were really the Christian god, it would be better to worship the Zeus of Paestum.

All this and a great deal more the Irish boy said, as he stood staring with disgust at Michelangelo's 'Moses'.

There seemed to be a danger that if he were asked to accept the Old Testament even as the necessary foundation for the Christian story, he might give up his search, or conduct it only in the Diocletian baths. We admitted that the tribal deity of the Hebrews was in part an evil conception, and agreed that to read about it had had a disastrous effect on the English people. But that was a Protestant emphasis, and in the 'low churches' they even substitute Old Testament psalms for the songs of the Blessed Virgin and of Simeon, so intense is their dislike of the doctrine of the Incarnation, the descent of the Spirit into matter and the redemption of the natural world. They may accept it theoretically, in the same way that Catholics accept theoretically beliefs in which they show little conviction, but they do not like it. In Calvinist Scotland the great midwinter feast is not the Birth of Christ but New Year's Day. The most extreme Protestants of all reject it entirely, and allow no sanctification of material things. Oddly enough this gives them a complete mastery of those things, no longer dedicated to God, and they amass large fortunes, free even of the claims of charity, like the rich tourist at Amalfi. For amongst large groups of Protestants, poverty is evidence of sin, and in the 1870's no one was admitted to S. Paul's Cathedral unless he was smartly dressed ; and Roger Fry's pious parents forbade him to give sixpence to a poor man, sitting by a frozen pond, who helped him on with his skates.

Worse even than this, though related to it, is the belief of Calvin and Luther that man is not merely imperfect, a drawing to be corrected, but evil in his essential nature, and so they do not look to the Perfection of Christ to redeem them, but only to his death, the blood sacrifice offered to the savage nostrils of the tribal god whom they regard most. They condemn any reverence for the Blessed Virgin, not because it is idolatrous, but because it brings kindness and the beauty of human life into our worship. Even so, we should remember that it is the Evangelical Nonconformists who most clearly affirm Christian values in England today.

But we are in Italy. Our search is amongst Catholic noumena, and we do not have to consider these things, as Catholics accept the first statement of the gospel, that it is to the poor.

'But Catholics also believe in the Old Testament,' said the Irish boy, 'or they wouldn't keep this horrible statue in a church.'

There were many things in churches that are inherited, some of great artistic value, which could not all suddenly be removed, even if they are inconsistent with the Church's teaching. Catholicism probably contains most of the doctrines, or the germ of them, that we dislike in Protestantism, but the emphasis is different. They regard the Old Testament as the basis of the New, but superseded. They sing in thousands of churches every day, all over the world, as we heard at Amalfi :

> Et antiquum documentum
> Novo cedat ritui.

One cannot emphasize this too much. Christ wiped out the Old Testament in a sentence, even the law of Moses, when

he said : 'The Sabbath was made for man', and he rubbed
the corn of Ceres in his hands.

But even the law of Moses was a necessary foundation for
our conduct. We can accept it, without the part about graven
images, which could hardly be taken seriously in Rome.

'Why could not Christ have been born amongst the
Greeks ?' asked the Irish boy.

We are not theologians and could not pretend to understand the motives of the Supreme Nóos, but we suggested it
was because there was a kind of singleness of purpose amongst
the Jews which was not found amongst the Greeks. In the
psalms is the universal sorrow and aspiration of the human
soul, the longing of the hart for the waterbrooks. There is
also, in spite of the blood sacrifices, that insistence on the
loving-kindness of God in the Old Testament. He was groaning and travailing to reveal himself to fallen man. In the Old
Testament he only partly got through, and the evil noumena,
the devils, revealed themselves with almost equal force. But
persisting through it all was the echo of loving-kindness, and
a unity of moral principle ; and as the rose has to be grafted
on to the rough stock of the briar, so Christ had to be grafted
on to a strong single stem. But when we have grafted the
rose we have to be careful to cut back any shoots that come
from the briar stock, which will bear no flowers. The Protestants refuse to do this, so that the true rose is choked with
useless wood.

It is true that Christ accepted the mythology of his day.
He was not a theologian but a revelation of the beauty and
wisdom of God, and theologians, like scientists, are far removed from the apprehension of beauty. They try with their
intellects to define the infinite. Christ revealed it through
poetry, through the art of his illustrations. He could not
have begun revising the Hebrew system of theology. He
came to fulfil what was true in it and to let the rest die off.
Occasionally, as we have seen, he dismissed it in a few words.

And so it is through our eyes and our hearts that we try to apprehend him, and even this Moses had acted as a wholesome purgative. It has cleared out what we cannot digest.

Still, this was rather a negative experience and the Irish boy was anxious to find more evidence of the good noumena to encourage him in his search. We left the church, and after a conversation with a young Cambridge graduate who was selling postcards to enable himself to live in Rome, we went down to the Colosseum, and took an 86 bus to S. Giovanni Laterano.

We went first into the octagonal baptistery, once the nymphaeum of the Lateran palace, where there are bronze doors from the Baths of Caracalla. Here a priest was christening a baby, and the man with the *New Statesman* who was watching said : 'Poor kid !' It did not seem to us unfortunate to begin life by being admitted to the blessed company of all faithful people, here in the Cathedral of Christendom, on the very spot where the Emperor Constantine had been baptized sixteen hundred years earlier.

'It has a good place in history,' said the Irish boy ; but the man with the *New Statesman* only looked contemptuous and went away.

In the cathedral we met some friends who told us that a monsignor was about to show them the crypt, a great and rare privilege. We were included in the invitation. It was a hot day, and at first the coolness of these vaults was grateful, but after three hours, while it was explained to us which of these layers of earthy bricks were part of the Lateran family's house, and which part of the basilica of Sylvester, we began to shiver in our thin clothes, and looking up through the small round gratings in the floor of the church, we had glimpses of the glorious renascence ceiling far above us in another world, gold and blue and crimson like the ceiling of heaven, and our little group of archaelogical pilgrims were like souls in an icy purgatory. We were released in the late afternoon and went across to the Santa Scala. Again the antique glaze had come with the low sun, and looking back at the great west front of the church, the soaring statues, the Theban obelisk — the oldest of all — against the long low building with a belfry beyond, we saw a Rome which conformed with part of our earliest imagination.

The Santa Scala, the marble stairs from Pilate's palace, were brought from Jerusalem by S. Helena, and now, with the Sanctus Sanctorum chapel at the top, are all that is left of the Lateran palace, where Pope Leo III crowned Charlemagne, taking him unawares, the first omen of the medieval theocratic society. These are the stairs that Christ mounted to his trial, and this does not seem improbable. Pilate's palace would be more easily identified than the manger at Bethlehem ; but even assuming — to please those sceptics who are inclined to believe that every object of Christian veneration is fraudulent (though Lenin's old overcoat is venerated in Moscow, and an air-marshal's hat in an English R.A.F. college) — that these are not Pilate's stairs, if for sixteen hundred years people have believed that on them a god, who was also the perfection of humanity, mounted to suffer insult and torture from those who could not endure his splendour, and with hearts full of shame and sorrow have climbed them on their knees, from that fact alone, apart from any original authenticity, they have become sacred. Here, on 19 September 1870, the eve of the *dies irae*, when the princes who from the beginning had warred against the Church, struck, as it seemed, their final blow, and turned the centre of Christendom, the capital of the Western world, into the capital of just another European kingdom, Pio Nono 'with abundance of tears' ascended these holy steps ; perhaps an unconscious act of penitence for all the crimes of the papacy, which, through this symbolic death to the world and to temporal power, was to rise to greater spiritual authority than it had ever known. For today the Pope alone, of all the rulers whose utterances are broadcast round the world, speaks with unalterable moral conviction, and with the wisdom that is drawn from the deep wells of Christian truth. This the Irish boy accepts as a mere statement of fact. It is certainly not true of anyone else.

Pio Nono is buried in the crypt of S. Lorenzo fuori le Mura, a basilica ordered by Constantine, but curiously joined to another church built by Sixtus III. It still has splendid antique columns and mosaics, though on 19 July 1943 it was bombed by the Allies. In the porch is a tablet which records how on that day there appeared among the ruins 'il Pastore Angelico, Pio XII, che inesauribile di aiuto e di conforto per i deboli, vindice del diritto presso i forti . . . con parole potente serene illuminatrice . . . la sua Roma salvo dell' estrema rovina'. He drove there alone and prayed in the shattered church, and it must have been on his return that he wrote that memorable letter to the Archdeacon of Rome, which, published to the world, was a breath of sanity in the welter of destruction, which should earn the 'imperishable gratitude' not only of the Romans who gave this tablet, but of all those who find in Rome the capital of their civilization, that 'pure word' of Turgenev. So after the tears of Pio Nono, and a brief ineffectual attempt to save the city with guns, it was saved from a far worse fate by the calm and powerful words alone of Pio Dodicesimo.

The Irish boy, who at first had watched with a faint, almost derisive smile, the pilgrims climbing the stairs on their knees, after these reflections had an attitude of greater respect, but he did not feel inclined to do it himself, nor yet would he cheat by walking up one of the side stairs, to see the picture of Christ by S. Luke, painted with the help of the holy angels, or as we would say, with the help of the noumena. This is not miraculous to us, as we have agreed that any picture not painted with the help of the holy angels is not a work of art.

From the Santa Scala we went to S. Croce in Gerusalemme,

F

where there is the relic of the True Cross, also brought to Rome by S. Helena, as the result of a vision. As we walked down the Viale Carlo Felice, the Irish boy said : 'I don't like all this preoccupation with death. The Apollo of Veii and the Apollo of Tevere are full of life, but the face of Christ is always tortured. The other day one of those Catholic hell-cat writers wrote that the Christian religion is concerned not with life but with death. If that is true, I'd rather go back to Paestum.'

We pointed out that those who he alleged were Catholic hell-cat writers were not the official voice of the Church. Those in England were mostly converts who found themselves in an equivocal position, repudiating the right of private judgment, but having themselves exercised it at their conversion. They are seldom at ease in their new home. The late Father John Talbot said : 'Never sneer at the Anglicans. That's what the converts do.' When a monsignor made an unfortunate public statement, a Roman Catholic lady said to us : 'Thank Heaven, he's a convert.' So in a kind of perverse fury, enjoying the only pleasure left to them, *le plaisir de déplaire*, they try to make their religion sound as repulsive to reason and humanity as possible. Continental Catholics, practising the natural religion of their country, are infinitely more gracious and charitable, whatever the official dogma may be. The choir from S. Stephen's, Vienna, sing in King's Chapel in Cambridge. It is impossible to imagine the choir of Westminster Cathedral doing this.

All the same we had to admit that in Christianity of every kind, not only Catholic, there was far more preoccupation with death than we cared for, and we did not accept it. It had resulted in what Miss Stevie Smith calls 'the sweet-cruel religion of Europe' and 'a sort of Christianity — sweet, cruel, dramatic, and R.C. — which many writers have made us familiar with'. This is what Turgenev called 'the anti-human side of a religion that should have been full of love and mercy'.[1] Anglicans frequently talk of 'the challenge of sin and suffering'.   They might as well talk of the challenge of bad drainage when they have a superb Titian hanging over their mantelpiece.   It is the splendour of God which is the challenge, if they must use that kind of language, not the wounds he has suffered from evil forces.   The challenge is from heavenly beauty, not from disease and death, and our courage shows in how we respond to the magnificence of the Supreme Nóos and his glorious Son in human flesh, in how we try to distinguish his beauty and save it from the injuries it has suffered, not to gloat over the injuries, the blood, the wounds, and the nails.   In a French church we once saw a litany called : 'Invocations à Jésus outragé dans sa Face adorable'.   It compared him to all the beauties of the natural world, the flowers in the hedgerows, and so was a true expression of the Incarnation, and it is perhaps that Face, behind the outrages, that we are seeking.

So when we arrived at S. Croce in Gerusalemme, the Irish boy was not in the mood to venerate relics of the Passion.   He said : 'I don't believe that it's the true Cross, anyhow.'

It may not be, but, as with the Santa Scala, if it has been venerated as such by devout pilgrims for many centuries, it has acquired sanctity, and the noumena of expiation have gathered around this piece of wood.   Mr. Aldous Huxley expounds this theory in *The Perennial Philosophy*, the most convincing book in our limited reading, even if we do not accept all its conclusions, of the existence of forces behind matter and able to control it.

We came out of the chapel of the True Cross into a passage where, behind a sheet of glass let into the wall, is a piece of the cross of the dying thief.   Just then a party of boys entered in charge of a priest.   They appeared to be ordinary healthy boys from twelve to fifteen years old ; then we saw that they were all deaf and dumb.   One of them kissed his

[1] *Turgenev.* David Magarshack.

fingers and pressed them against the glass in the wall. The Irish boy watched him, and his look of scepticism faded, and the tears came into his eyes. The dumb boy, too, was the victim of evil noumena, and Apollo was unable to help him. He needed the cross for his consolation, and in his humility only dared to touch that of the dying thief.

CHAPTER VI

THREE PICTURES

THE next day the Irish boy said that he had had as much ecclesiology as he could assimilate for the time being, and we went to the Borghese Gallery to look at some pictures. As we crossed the dry grass under the trees, and entered the ochre-washed palace, glowing like a lovely renascence jewel in the afternoon sun, we decided, following our exclusive plan, to look at only three, and went straight to the first of them, Caravaggio's 'Madonna della Serpe', at the south end of the long middle gallery upstairs.

We had to wait, as here again, standing before it, was the man with the *New Statesman* in his pocket. His grim, boyish, wistful face looked more cross than usual, as it was difficult to attune his aesthetic responses both to Caravaggio, who is now fashionable, and to the jigsaw puzzles of Picasso. He is still seeking salvation in 'culture', and he knows that to be cultured he has to perform this intellectual gymnastic, which is only possible by depriving everything of meaning. There are no noumena. In a picture nothing must appeal to the heart or mind. He can only wait for the tactile sensations in his finger-tips, which is why he stands so long before the Madonna. He is not happy as he wanders round Rome where everything is potent with meaning ; where all the accretions in our Western souls continually sparkle like Stendhal's crystals, reflecting the light that formed them ; where works of passionate beauty have been created with the heart's blood. 'It all seems dead to me,' he says, and he goes often to look at the new railway station, which certainly is light and splendid.

He has lost God and therefore he has lost nature. 'It is

difficult and dangerous', said Goethe, 'to think separately of
God and Nature. It is as if we should think separately of the
body and the soul.' This is the doctrine of the Incarnation.
According to another noted critic, nature, formerly an 'enclosed garden' to mankind, has been shown by science to be
hostile and cruel. Because of this the artist can no longer paint
the Perugino hill-side, the streams and the vineyards, and the
loveliness of the human face — only horrors, abstract designs,
and distortions. Apparently the primrose, the nightingale,
ferns, and skipping lambs are only the invention of Victorian
lady water-colourists, and are no design of the super-hell-
fiend who created the monstrous and diabolical world in which
we are forced to endure our terrifying existence. This may
be true to a few scientists and neurotic intellectuals. It is
nonsense to those with unperverted minds. The office worker
and the city child long to escape to the country, their natural
home, for restoration and peace. It is no more hostile to them
than their own dwellings because some criminal lunatic, armed
with weapons devised by ingenious moral imbeciles, may
blow the whole thing up. The possibility only makes it more
passionately dear. We have conquered most of such dangers
as threatened us from the natural world. Those that remain
come from our own distorted natures. Was the world more
an 'enclosed garden' to S. Catherine, voyaging in a tiny ship
through Mediterranean storms, or tramping the stony mountains to Avignon, a journey we make in a night in a sleeper;
or was it more so to those who ran, *eheu fugaces*, from the
destruction of Pompeii?

These unhappy people who see the willows by the stream
as a menace, and the human face distorted, chopped up into
mechanical planes, elongated or forming a senseless design,
have lost the noumena which alone can create a work of art.
Worse, they have lost from their hearts the image of the Perfect Drawing. Yet they remain aware that they themselves
are only rough sketches drawn by night. They are Caliban

enraged at seeing nothing but his own face in the glass, and
finding their imperfection intolerable, like a petulant child
which has splashed its new dress and then jumps farther into
the mud to make it entirely filthy, they try to escape their
humiliation by distorting their reflections still further, and
declaring that evil is good.

Yet even the bad noumena seem to have deserted them.
There is no sap even in their evil. They are so completely
sterile that when they want to shock they have to copy the
degenerate nightmares of Bosch and Grünewald, painted at a
time when the evil in the Gothic world had turned the flame
of its aspiration into foul smoke, and Apollo had not yet risen
again from the Tiber. Though they may claim that their
work is the result of unfettered imagination, magic from the
subconscious, which suggests the influence of the noumena,
it is only the imagination of an uncontrolled mind. The heart,
equally necessary to creation, has no part in it.

The man with the *New Statesman* in his pocket is clearly
stricken with this death, which has come to him from his
puritan ancestors, for the puritan has always accepted the
wicked view of the natural world which we have indicated ;
not only because he denies the descent of the spirit into matter,
but because he has been conditioned to believe that what is
hard and cruel and hostile to human tenderness is good for the
soul, though it is only in this tenderness that our love of the
good can take root. He sees the wonders of creation redeemed
by Christ as distorted and hostile, and the Mother and Child
as a stone with holes in it. The curse of Descartes seems to
have come not only on science but on art itself. The universe
has become dumb.

At last this poor heir of death, with his weekly bible in
his pocket, moved away from the Caravaggio. He did not
look as if his finger-tips, or indeed any part of his anatomy,
were tingling very much.

Ourselves standing before this painting, full of the sharp

and sombre power which is in nearly all Caravaggio's work,
were aware of tactile sensations, but we took them more or
less for granted. We wanted to know what it meant. The
Blessed Virgin has her bare foot on the head of a horribly
alive, writhing snake. She is holding the boy Christ, who,
naked and innocent, places his foot on her own, while S. Anne
watches, with the patient detachment, the sympathy modified
by wisdom, with which old people see the struggles and
endurance of the young. It is surely a vision of the anguish
inevitable in the Incarnation, apart from the Crucifixion.
That third part of the Supreme Nóos which was love, having
entered a human body, in his childhood had to learn to endure
the pain which the contact of his perfection with our imperfection brings him. This he does at first through the flesh
of his mother, who puts her own foot between his and the
head of the snake. His forehead is puckered with distaste, and
yet a certain firmness in his body shows that he accepts his
lot. This picture may be a justification for the place of the
Immaculate Conception in the Story, for how could he, in
his first sensitive youth, endure the contact with evil except
through the flesh of innocence?

Caravaggio was a complete blackguard. Among other
things he murdered his mistress and used her corpse as a model.
Yet because of this, like a Dostoevsky character, he may have
had far more understanding of the contact between evil and
good than the more respectable ; and he used his tormented
heart, as well as his head, in creation.

Our next picture was Jacopo da Bassano's 'L' Ultima
Cena', which takes up nearly a whole wall in a small room at
the north-west corner of the palace. It is an extraordinary
painting, which it is possible at a first glance to see almost as
'amusing'. Perhaps it is a little amusing because of its touches
of ordinary life — the untidy supper table, the half-eaten piece
of bread, the apple with its leaf attached, the dog lying beside
the copper preserving-pan on the floor, the knife about to fall

as the disciple on the left rumples up the cloth in the excitement of his argument. In the centre of the picture is Christ,
his hand outstretched to an almost surrealist sheep's head on
the table. Before him, his cheek supported on his hand, is
S. John the beloved disciple, the bored drowsy boy, but con-
tent to be resting close to his god, who stands serene, aloof,
pensive, while all around the heated disputatious men try with
their limited brains to arrive at the exact definition of truth.
Not one of them is looking where it is revealed, love sleeping
against the breast of wisdom, a few feet from them. Not one
of them is using his heart or his eyes. This picture is an
allegory of the history of the Church, especially as Judas has
not yet left them, but is standing behind on the extreme right,
pondering with the expression of a dishonest dealer.

F. D. Maurice — in this scene he is almost as surrealist as
the sheep's head — told Charles Kingsley that it was quite
wrong to paint S. John as a fresh and innocent youth. He was
the disciple whom Christ loved, and love, said Maurice, gives
a face lined and furrowed with anxiety at the evil conditions
under which men live — slum dwellings, inadequate sanitation, the unequal distribution of wealth. It is possible that
he confused love with a strong sense of justice combined with
moral indignation. These may be noble, but they are not the
love that Christ had for S. John, who is Eros redeemed. His
love was for the beauty of mankind, and was perhaps necessary
to his human nature to enable it to love entirely the human
race. How could he, knowing all things — not in his mind,
which had accepted the limitations of his time, but in his
heart — have endured all those disputatious apostles, without
the presence of that sleepy trusting youth, who also knew
only in his heart, who 'still is nature's priest' ?

There are ascetics who say that if someone young and
attractive asks for our help, we should be inclined to refuse,
as we only give for our own pleasure. This is devil-worship,
for by nature and by Christ himself we are taught to love

what is young and beautiful — all those Leonardo faces in the streets of Rome, and the vital Bronzinos, the seraphic pieces of life and the tumbling jewels. Those whom Christ looked on and loved were certainly in their first sparkling life, in the fullness of their strength and yet innocent, close to the gates of Paradise. In them it seems more possible that the sketch can be changed to the Perfect Drawing. A story in which there is no place for the Ephebe of Subiaco, or for this drowsy boy, cannot be the basis of a civilization worthy of the name. He is at the heart of the Greek and the Gospel stories, and at mass the acolyte who serves the priest is S. John in 'L' Ultima Cena'.

Our third picture, which satisfies Turgenev's condition, is in the next room. It is Correggio's 'Danae'. This is sheer golden loveliness, a pagan story with no meaning beyond that of its own beauty. Here there is no bitter contact between good and evil, no contrast between the nagging intellect and serene wisdom. There is not even an awareness of evil or sign of its existence, though the subject is pagan, and to the puritan immoral. Danae is on her bed, and Eros helps her to prepare for the golden rain, about to burst from the soft cloud above. Two *putti* in the corner are engrossed in their own affairs, being occupied with a paint-brush, perhaps mixing the paints, which might well have been done by such *amorini*. Their presence and their indifference fills the whole scene with innocence. There is a hint of solid animal flesh in the arm of Eros, but otherwise the picture, though pagan, gives the feeling of 'light through'. It could only have been painted after centuries of Christian belief, and from it again we have that satisfaction which comes when we find the two Stories blended into one. The gold is not so much in the colour, which is tender and subdued, as a feeling in the air. Lyricism has become hushed, and attentive to truth.

CHAPTER VII

PAULUS EXCLUSUS—QUO VADIS?

As the Irish boy was shortly to come up against his stiffest hurdle, we prolonged our interlude, and for the next two or three days went to bathe at Fregene, where there is a long sandy beach at the edge of a pine wood. Here we lunched out of doors and drank the delicious white wine grown at Maccarese, only two miles away, and worshipped, in fact if not in word, the Ephebe of Subiaco, for people in their deeds are all day unconsciously worshipping something, Apollo or Bacchus or most often and most respectably the Golden Calf.

We went to Fregene by bus from the Porta Flaminia. Coming back, our bus raced furiously with five others swaying along the narrow road. When we mentioned this to an Italian friend, he told us that the ambition of every Italian young man is to be a racing motorist, and that those who cannot afford it take jobs as bus drivers to release their repressions.

In these three days of healthy, sun-drenched animal life, our minds were cured of the vicious habit of over-cerebration, which was a danger of our search, its occupational disease. The Irish boy's eyes were fresh for new sights, and his heart in a healthy condition of responsiveness. So we went to S. Paolo fuori le Mura.

This church is about a mile or more beyond the Porta S. Paolo, along a dusty road with commercial buildings and trams. It is enormous and mostly new, though it was first built by the Emperor Constantine over the tomb of the apostle, still under the high altar. It was enlarged, rebuilt, and adorned by various emperors and popes, until in A.D.

1823 it all went up in flames, which must have been something of a miracle, for how can bronze and marble burn ?

It was built to its former design, an amazing achievement for the nineteenth century. It is like a vast hall of justice, with its eighty huge marble pillars, and the effect is increased by the great statues of S. Paul in the forecourt and in the church, holding his forbidding sword and book. No one is praying in this church. There is nowhere inviting prayer. The chapels at the east end are shut off behind glass and screens. The extremely Roman-Catholic-looking body of Blessed Placidus Riccardi, on which the statue of the apostle looks down with pinched nostrils of distaste, is the only striking reminder in this place of the future life. For Henry Wotton's lines might as well have been written here, as of S. Paul's in London :

> St. Paul's, beneath whose ample dome
> No thought arises of the things to come.

S. Paul is 'the Protestant saint', and it is surprising how in his church the material things symbolize with the spirit. Is it intentional ? Did the noumenon of S. Paul, haunting the place, prohibit the architects from introducing that humanity which is the message of the Incarnation ? There are no *putti*, no consoling images. The pulpit, surely the only one in Rome made of that polished mahogany used so much in banks, faces straight down the church, as in an English nonconformist chapel, and more conspicuous than the altar is the throne, flanked by huge pillars, like that of a menacing judge.

We went through into the fine cloisters which escaped the fire of 1823, but even here the noumenon of S. Paul has expressed itself. The first thing we saw on the walls was the Roman *fasces* — again the hall of justice. In the cloister garth, instead of the box-hedges, the weeds amongst the cobbles, the few casual flowers which might have been picked for a

wreath for the Esquiline Aphrodite, or for a tight childish
bunch for the Madonna, there are orderly rose beds, fit for a
rich business man's garden at Wimbledon. In the middle,
instead of a fountain splashing gently from a mossy stone
dolphin, there is a neat, white-marble basin with a chromium-
plate fitting, and even more symbolic, it is without water.
More surprising still, opening off the lovely cloisters are
modern well-equipped lavatories ; and on this day, still more
appropriate, the tourists buying souvenirs at the stall had
Midland accents.

The Irish boy, instead of approving of all this absence of
superstition, felt that the emanations of the place were almost
frighteningly consistent, as if the most grim Protestant noumena had discovered our flirtation with Catholic paganism,
and had gathered in strength to forbid it ; so we left the
church and went across to an open-air stall, to drink orangeade
under some stunted, dusty pine trees. We sat there for an
hour, discussing S. Paul.

The Irish boy had just realized that the unspeakable boredom he felt in church as a child was caused as much by the
epistles of S. Paul as by the Old Testament. He instinctively
rejected them. The discovery of the cause of his distaste had
suddenly come to him, giving him a sense of freedom, which
he used to state his repudiation of that apostle.

When a saint is canonized, he said, someone is appointed
to act as 'Devil's Advocate' to rake up everything possible to
the candidate's discredit, so that no unworthy person may be
placed in the Calendar. S. Paul presumably had never been
'screened' by a Devil's Advocate, and he was now going to
perform the function. The Irish boy was still provisionally
a free-thinker, and he saw no reason to qualify his remarks
from motives of reverence. As in places they were ribald,
we shall paraphrase them to avoid giving offence to those who
hold more orthodox views.

First of all, he drew attention to Paul before his conversion.

We admitted at Paestum that the pagan gods have to be redeemed, also that the pagan gods are little more than our own
natures. When they are redeemed they are still the same,
but illuminated. What was S. Paul's nature ? We read that
'he made havoc of the church, entering into every house, and
haling men and women, committed them to prison'. Also
he was 'breathing threatenings and slaughter against the
disciples'. He was evidently a bigot, a self-important bully,
and even a murderer. The first Christian to be killed for
his belief was at his direction. He witnessed the murder
complacently.

Then, he tells us, he had that moment of illumination,
which was a direct command from God. We have only his
own authority for it, and such a story would not be accepted
today by an Anglican bishop. But, assuming it was genuine,
how did he behave ? The innocent Son of God, to strengthen
himself for his work on earth, went into the wilderness to
endure the three temptations. What expiation should not
Paul have undergone before he dared to preach the merciful
gospel of Christ ? Surely after his vision he should have gone
into the wilderness for years to recondition his savage nature ?
But with his hands still wet with the blood of Stephen, with
the cries of the women he had dragged to prison still in his
ears, he just stepped over and continued his activities, still
self-righteous, in the other camp.

Here we interrupted the Devil's Advocate to point out
not only S. Paul's splendid courage, but that he broke the
close Jewish walls that some of the disciples would have kept
round the Christian religion, and let it flow out over the whole
Gentile world ; that if it were not for him we should not
even have the option of becoming Christians.

The Irish boy retorted that Pauline Christianity was not
that of the gospels. One did not need to be a literary critic
to see the difference. Christ is the Second Adam who came
to our rescue. He does not want to destroy our pleasures but

to restore them to innocence. His first miracle was to turn water, not merely into wine, but into very good wine. He hardly makes one exact theological statement. He teaches people how to feel, not how to think. He walks in the fields and says : 'The Sabbath was made for man', wiping out the Law and the whole legalistic wrangle. He says : 'Consider the lilies.' All his images are taken from the natural world. He loves children. He has that urbane, almost worldly conversation with the loose woman at the well. He says : 'Neither do I condemn thee' to the adulteress. He says : 'Take no thought for the morrow.' He says nothing about the obligation of earning one's living, knowing that the idle may love God, and there is no suggestion that he did a day's work in his life. He allowed a woman to pour expensive scent on his feet, and he wore a seamless garment. He had no respect for ecclesiastical authority — in fact, a violent contempt. He did not bother to answer God's high priest. When he attacks, it is sometimes with just anger, 'Woe unto you', and sometimes with a piercing, almost cynical, wit, which Western theologians have tormented themselves in trying to interpret literally. 'It is easier for a camel to go through a needle's eye' is almost American in its pungency. So is 'Make to yourselves friends of the Mammon of unrighteousness.' He is not only the Prince of Heaven, but in his humanity also a prince, debonair, courteous, contemptuous only of the pompous and the cruel, and compassionate to the truly poor, the afflicted and distressed.

'Now let us consider the bourgeois S. Paul,' said the Devil's Advocate. 'Not in his original state of vile cruelty before his conversion, but when he claims to have turned from his wickedness, and to be the apostle of the Light.'

We have read somewhere that he worked amongst 'the urban middle classes'.[1] In all his writings there are implications

[1] *S. Catherine of Siena*, Sigrid Undset.

favourable to them, whereas the sayings and behaviour of
Christ are hostile to a respectable society. When Christ
says : 'My kingdom is not of this world', he does not mean
that it is not of the innocent natural world created by his
Father, but of the social and economic world, the world of
oppression and of the Golden Calf. S. Paul, like a good
bourgeois, urges obedience to the state, without any qualification. That is an essential difference between him and Christ,
but there are others more fundamental.

He had never, like the other apostles, known Christ, and
so could not understand his teaching or his nature in the
same way that those who had lived with him daily for three
years understood it. Because of this disability whenever he
mentions him, he at once kills him and turns him into a
complete myth, the victim in the blood sacrifice. He preaches
Christ Crucified. He does not preach Christ alive on this
earth, in all the splendour of his innocent humanity. He
never once mentions his sayings or his deeds. Compare
them with those we have just mentioned. Where are the
lilies and the corn, the children and the conversations with
loose women ? Where is the indifference to theology, the
contempt for lawyers, and the forgiving of the disreputable ?
Those who resist the power of the state :

'Shall receive to themselves damnation.'

'God shall smite thee, thou whited wall !'

'If ye have no chastisement then are ye bastards.'

'Alexander the coppersmith did me much evil.'

'Hymenaeus and Alexander whom I have delivered unto
Satan that they may learn not to blaspheme.' The text for
the Inquisition.

He quarrelled with Barnabas, the Son of Consolation, with
whom surely it must have been difficult to pick a quarrel.
Compare all this with the 'Catholic' epistle of S. James,
the care for the poor and the orphaned children, the references to the flowers of the grass and the fruit of the olive

tree, the gentleness. And Paul's boasting. He is surrounded by the devils of the Third Temptation. Like a good bourgeois, he boasts that he earns his living, and that he was Roman born. Even the reason for 'patient continuance in well-doing' is not a selfless love of the Perfect Drawing, but the bourgeois rule of fair returns, 'glory and honour and immortality'. It is sheer commercial calculation. He boasts : 'Henceforth there is laid up for me a crown of righteousness.' He boasts of his sufferings and imprisonments. He boasts that he persecuted the Church, and we only loudly confess the sins of which we are secretly proud. Is not even the famous thirteenth chapter of Corinthians one long implied boast, that he has all the virtues which are nothing without love. How much simpler to say : 'He that loveth not his brother whom he hath seen, how can he love God whom he hath not seen ?' again the doctrine of the Incarnation, which Paul could not preach as he had not seen God in the flesh, and his Old Testament imagination was steeped in the idea of blood sacrifice.

We pointed out that the saints themselves are only rough sketches drawn by night, that it is impossible to compare even the best of them with the Perfect Drawing. One cannot compare a man with a divine revelation.

'Yes,' said the Devil's Advocate, 'but the true self of every man is a divine revelation. Even so, my objection is not to his imperfection, but to his regarding it as perfection. He had no idea what the Perfect Drawing looked like. Can you imagine him talking by a well, with a woman who had had five husbands, without becoming choleric with denunciation ? He told Timothy to allow no women under sixty into his circle, as they might marry again. He would have excluded the Blessed Virgin herself, who could not have been sixty at the time of the Crucifixion, when Christ with love gave her into the care of the sleepy boy in "L' Ultima Cena", as she had no other sons.'

G

All the same, we objected, he led a heroic life, and spread Christianity through the Greek and Roman world, and consequently to ourselves.

'But what sort of Christianity?' asked the Devil's Advocate. 'Not that of the Gospels, breathing of humanity and the scents of the fields. Something has happened to it. "Each thing here is partly true and partly false. Essential truth is not so; it is altogether pure and altogether true. This mixture dishonours and annihilates it." [1]   S. Paul had mixed the Gospel truth. He has taken it and given it a medicated flavour, as the bees do, when they fuss busily about the garden; but Christ is the pure honey from the calyx of the flower.'

*

We had no reply, and the Irish boy resumed his own personality. He still continued to discuss the great church across the road, beyond the tram-lines. Why was this, he asked, S. Paul's only church in Rome, outside the walls? The Catholics may have to accept him, but they cannot like him. No one lights him a candle, or brings him flowers, for who could bring flowers to this angry face, this unkempt beard, and the huge threatening sword?

Here it is easy to believe in the power of the noumena over material substances, for surely the noumenon of S. Paul could not have expressed itself more suitably than in that great soulless judgment hall. And did the noumena of Catholic and pagan Rome insist that the father of Protestantism should stay without the walls? Did they even burn it down, for how, as we asked before, could this bronze and marble burn, except by miraculous intervention?

The Irish boy, in spite of the wine of Maccarese and the strengthening suns of Fregene, or perhaps because of them, could not take the hurdle of S. Paul. He had walked round it,

---

[1] *Pensées*, Pascal.

and we rose to return within the walls. Our *aranciata* was
twenty lire more a glass than elsewhere.

'The proprietor evidently belongs to the urban middle
classes,' said the Irish boy.

★

We did not return directly to Rome, but walked, by some
more or less country roads, across to the Appian Way and the
neighbourhood of the catacombs. Having seen enough of
these tunnels at S. Agnese, we walked on until we came to a
place called 'Quo Vadis Domine ?' In the church is a stone
with a footmark on it. A girl in charge of the place pointed
at it and said 'Cristo'. Here, we are told, S. Peter, fleeing
from death, was met by Christ, and asked him : 'Where
are you going, Lord ?' Christ replied : 'I am going to Rome
to be crucified again in your place'. S. Peter was so ashamed
that he returned and suffered a terrible death, where Bramante
has built his serene little temple. The Irish boy did not mind
about the possibly fraudulent footprint. It may have been
carved with no intent to deceive, simply as an indication at a
time when people could not read ; but he was furious at the
wicked legend.

The evil noumenon, he said, whom in the Story we call
the devil, terrified by the Incarnation of the Second Adam,
through whom man can be restored to equal innocence, did
all he could to smear and blot out the vision of his Face, and
confuse our conception of his nature. According to medieval
legend, the devil often took on himself the appearance of
Christ or an angel. He did so here, for what is the implication
of this tale ? It is that God, the loving Father preached by
Christ, demands the savour of blood and torture from his
children. Suffering has become not only something for which
we must be prepared as an inevitable consequence of opposition
to the values of this world, but is given an independent virtue
of its own, so that would-be saints cultivated self-injury and

disease. Why should the Supreme Nóos wish his good
creation to be blighted ? 'Suffering and disease are *not* the
will of God,' declared Bishop Gore, who presumably was
orthodox. Why should Christ, who spent his time on earth
healing sickness and relieving suffering, as soon as he returned
to Heaven inflict it as a mark of his love? A beautiful
woman who suffered disfigurement and agony from burns
was told by the nun who nursed her : 'How God must love
you!'

Here, at 'Quo Vadis Domine ?', is the beginning of the
'sweet cruelty' which has disfigured the religion of Europe,
the first picture of Christ as a kind of blackmailing governess,
with those horrible, soft, self-pitying, reproachful eyes. For
what would any decent man, let alone the noble Son of God,
say to a dear friend who had just escaped a cruel death ? He
would embrace him and exclaim : 'Thank Heaven you are
safe !' We cannot worship what is lower than ourselves.
This was the first victory of the devil after Calvary, and here
began the long process of turning the glorious Son of God —
Incarnate love, who walked through the corn, and blessed
the children, who pardoned the whore, and restored innocence
to the natural world — into the devil worshipped by Torquemada and Calvin. If you worship a fiend, even if you call
him by the name of God, he remains a fiend.

For God does not speak English, or Italian, or Latin, or
any other language. He does not even understand them.
When an Anglican clergyman goes down the aisle after the
anthem, and says in an earnest cultivated voice : 'We beseech
thee, O Lord, to improve the industrial situation, to endue
with good-will the employers and the dockers', there is no
echo in Heaven, except perhaps a dim faint note of good
intention. Neither the Supreme Nóos nor the lesser noumena
— the saints and angels — are attuned to that kind of sound.
They only feel the motions of the heart. We say prayers to
clarify and give shape to the desires of our hearts, and when

this is done they are in harmony with the noumena, who will influence matter according to our good desires. The monks who chant their offices, do so to get themselves into this condition. Their real prayers begin when the plainsong fades into silence ; though it is possible that certain sounds, such as plainsong itself, do invoke the noumena ; and Orientals, who are far more advanced in the art of spiritual contact than Westerners, achieve it through making certain sounds, but they are not intellectual sounds, like the prayers for the dockers. If the Anglican clergyman really felt the industrial situation to be one of the wounds of the Nóos, he would go and prostrate himself, with an abundance of tears, before an image of the Sacred Heart.

This is not to say that the prayers of peasants and simple people are not heard, as with them feeling and utterance are immediate, and not divided by the intellect ; but more educated people must first get rid of this division, in rapidly muttered prayers, incantations, incense, and the clanging of bells.

After these considerations we felt that we ourselves were using our tricky minds more than was allowable in our search, and might soon begin delivering people to Satan, so we took the 218 bus back to the Colosseum. It had been rather an unnerving day, and we walked down into the old town, to refresh our hearts and eyes before the Fountain of the Tortoises, the loveliest in Rome.

CHAPTER VIII

SOME ROMAN CLOISTERS

THE Irish boy was so easily stimulated to rather heated moral reflections, that we thought it necessary to have another interlude free from causes of provocation. After all, a pilgrimage is a form of pleasure as well as of piety, and in the Middle Ages often became more a pilgrimage to a madonna of flesh and blood than to one of carved and painted wood. We avoided this extreme, and for the next two days made a tour of the cloisters of Rome.

If the streets are noisy and dangerous, there is always one of these havens of silence fairly close. After collecting letters at S. Silvestro, one can walk a hundred yards or so up the Via Mercede to read them in the cloister of S. Andrea delle Fratte, that church with Borromini's curious campanile, like some elaborate toy, an inkpot, or an ornament for a dinner table. The brickwork of the central *massif* has never been covered with smooth stone, which enables us more clearly to grasp its basic design. The cloister is not one of the most impressive, like those of S. Giovanni Laterano and S. Paolo, though in a new country people would travel hundreds of miles to see it, but it is pleasant with its orange trees and cypresses, and quiet after the street. Here, as in so many places of its kind, a handful of children are pursuing the drama of their lives. They discuss some plan with a priest ; they scuffle and grab each other round the neck ; one carries a basket in at a mysterious door.

At S. Maria in Campo Marzo, on the other side of the Corso, there is a court exactly like the background of a seventeenth-century painting, and looking through a grille we saw another where two great spreading fig trees grow from a stone

pavement. The Irish boy said that it would be delightful to
have lunch under them, with a bottle of Maccarese, and to
talk there late into the afternoon. We pointed out that this
would almost certainly lead us into the sin of over-cerebration,
with which he reluctantly agreed.

In Trastevere, the most purely Italian quarter of Rome,
where invaders and tourists have left little mark, there seems
to be most ancient peace, partly because being poor, the
inhabitants can afford few motor bicycles. Walking along a
street here, we were accosted by a man seated outside a door.
He practically compelled us to come in, though we showed
the greatest reluctance, feeling from the urgency of his manner
and his assurances of the pleasure we should have, that the
place could be hardly respectable. It was the cloister of S.
Giovanni dei Genovesi, and in it was the pattern of the
Christian garden, and we exclaimed :

> O happy harbour of the saints !
> O sweet and pleasant soil !

It is not wild and pagan, with the illicit lilies of the bindweed
in the box-hedges, nor is it a capitalist garden like S. Paolo's,
with only hybrid rose-bushes growing in the bare earth. It
contains all kinds of beautiful life, scented roses, fine lilies and
pinks, but even the blades of grass seem individual and tended
with equal care and love, given moisture according to their
need. The man who led us in, and whom we so grossly mis-
judged, sees that it is good. He is full of childlike pride, as God
was proud when he saw the lovely world he had made. He
was so satisfied with our appreciation that he was indifferent to
the inevitable 100 lire. He was the true artist, willing to accept
payment for his work, but more anxious to have it appreciated.

He also showed us the church, and a painted rococo chapel,
which if only it had been French might have been the private
chapel of that lady who, finding a Bible on her bedside table,
exclaimed : 'Quel effroyable ton !'

Near S. Giovanni dei Genovesi is another cloister, with a little ancient church too poor to have suffered baroque attention, and so modest that we have even forgotten its name, but think it is S. Francesco. It has a wide garden full of vines and flowers and vegetables, and the convent of nuns seems to be some kind of alms-house, as old people were sitting about gossiping. Also near by is the court before S. Cecilia, a garden with a fountain. Although we were keeping the Irish boy away from churches for the present, we went in to see Maderna's statue of the saint under the altar, a strange and touching piece of realism. It is said to be an exact portrait of her body as it was found lying with, no taint of decay, when her tomb was opened at the end of the sixteenth century, thirteen hundred years after her death. We found the man with the *New Statesman* here, looking at it with disgust, as it has that tenderness which he cannot endure in any work of art. For he knows that he is empty in the middle. He has lost the noumenon which would enable him to support any feelings of compassion, and so if he were to let them penetrate his thin protective case of intellect, he would be utterly dissolved and ruined. This is not to say that he is without moral indignation. He simmers with it all the time, far more than the Irish boy. But it is a bewilderment to us, as it is unrelated to any moral system we have ever heard of. He was as indignant that a college garden had not been turned into a by-pass or a parking place, as if it had been discovered that the master of the college was a dope-peddler. He was indignant when the Irish boy said, with that mixture of piety and scepticism, reverence and irony, with which we make such statements : 'I have seen a piece of the manger from Bethlehem and a piece of the True Cross'. And yet he accepted every word written in the journal sticking out of his pocket as if it were the faith once for all delivered to the saints. He was furious that there should be the slightest check on divorce and abortion, as if in them alone lay the means of salvation. So, although we were sorry for him as he seemed lonely and a little blighted, we found conversation difficult with someone who took us into a kind of madhouse of moral values, and we went out again into the court.

It is enclosed at one end by the ancient Ionic columns of the portico, and on one side by a wall of syringa. It, too, is filled with roses and lilies. A friendly priest, with a pride as naïve but less importunate than that of the custodian of S. Giovanni, asked us if it was not beautiful. We were about to reply when there was an outburst of that vitality which seems continuous in Italian churches and cloisters. Three *putti* came dashing in from the piazza, and a child of eight flung himself into the arms of the priest. They all disappeared through one of those mysterious doorways. In a minute the child of eight returned with a large ball, and he raced back the way he had come, between the flower-beds, across the piazza he and the ball, bouncing, flying, parting, colliding in a weaving of design, until they passed from sight up a stairway on the other side. He was the infant Hermes, the quicksilver, the moving jewel tumbling in the street, the incarnation of the noumenon of his years ; so that if at any moment between his appearance in the atrium of S. Cecilia and his exit up the stairs he could have been frozen into stone, he would have formed an image of perfect grace, as eternal as the Ephebe of Subiaco, or the boy pulling out the thorn.

We did not in these two days necessarily visit the most famous and beautiful cloisters in Rome, some of which we had already seen — S. Giovanni Laterano with its twelfth-century double columns with barley-sugar twists, and, like the entablature above, decorated with gold mosaic ; S. Lorenzo fuori le Mura, which has the same atmosphere of extreme antiquity as the cloisters at Salerno and Amalfi ; the forecourt, the cypresses, and the steps of S. Gregorio Magno ; S. Clemente with its cobbles ; S. Paolo, also with twelfth-century double columns and its gentlemanly rose-garden. We

sought those that were less well known, where it was possible
to loiter undisturbed by tourists. It may seem ungrateful
therefore to direct tourists to them, but perhaps those who
may go as a result of reading this chapter will have more the
nature of pilgrims.

We returned across the river from Trastevere, on our way
to SS. Quattro Coronati, and passed the little round church
of S. Teodoro, one of the oldest in Rome, below the Palatine
hill. It looked deserted, inviting but impenetrable, which
made the Irish boy want to find a way in. We pointed out
that the small stone court, flanked by domestic buildings,
could not be called a cloister, and that churches alone were
for the present out of bounds. But a man from a workshop
across the road, with that unfailing Italian courtesy, came
over and showed us where to ring the bell, and we had to
enter. The custodian was delighted to have visitors, and with
equal enthusiasm showed us everything, the seventh-century
mosaics, some fairly modern paintings, but mostly bones.
The place has an air of great antiquity, due not to the mosaics
but to the neglect of the last fifty years. To convey antiquity
a place must suffer from present neglect. When it is well
cared for and tastefully arranged by modern experts, the
noumena are driven away, and we do not have that feeling
of dusty sadness which is so potent here, apart from the bones.
These are an astonishing collection. There is a finger of S.
Teodoro, and we were taken across the court to see some holy
skeletons. A kind of triptych behind an altar is like a biolo-
gist's specimen case. In twelve glass-fronted pigeon-holes are
twelve bits of bone, parts of the bodies of the twelve apostles.
Upstairs is more sad dust, rooms full of disused lockers and
cupboards and old prints.

'Look — cardinals !' exclaimed the custodian, seizing a
large cardboard sheet, covered with small eighteenth-century
prints of the princes of the Church, and almost obliterating
their features as he scrubbed away the dust.

When we left we felt sad at the thought of so much enthusiasm bound to so much decay, but the Irish boy was only indignant about the bones. 'Why do they keep all these bodies and bones ?' he asked. 'Perhaps the hell-cat writers are right, and Christianity is a religion of death.'

He said that most people die when they are fairly old. Even if they have not been martyred their bodies at the end caused them a fair amount of suffering and annoyance. They cannot see without their glasses and they are soon tired ; and these old saints lived before false teeth were invented, so they could not even enjoy a good dinner, the last pleasure of the old. They must be relieved to be finished with these worn-out conveniences which they inhabited. If they are saints they have gone to a region of light where it must be impossible to think of their old, aching bodies. It must be offensive and grotesque to them, who are now radiant heavenly beings, surrounded by beauty beyond our imagination, that people should preserve and venerate their old bones, or think of them as earth-bound spirits haunting these disgusting remains. When they were on earth they prayed : 'Grant that when our bodies lie in the dust, our souls may live with Thee.' Did people think that at the Resurrection all these scattered bits of bone would be reassembled and fastened on to their unfortunate radiant spirits ?

'Another thing,' he went on, 'Catholics won't let you be cremated because of the Resurrection, but that must be of your etheric body, or whatever the Spiritualists call it, not all these bones and corpses. And even if you are burnt you only turn into something else, like turning into grass when you're buried, and the grass may be mowed and burnt. So what then ? Also many of the martyrs were burned to death; the living torches lit by Nero. Are they excluded from Heaven ? And all those innocent children burned alive — rows of noughts — during the war ? Surely it is hard enough to adjust ourselves to the Perfect Drawing without the Church obscuring the image with sheer rot ?'

We refused to answer, as he had gone into a church outside our schedule ; and soon his attention was distracted by the apparent medieval fortress on the side of the Coelian hill, between S. Clemente and S. Giovanni Laterano.

It was SS. Quattro Coronati, the four brothers, officials who were flogged to death under Diocletian, and given martyrs' crowns. We climbed up some steps on to a small piazza and entered the first court. Before the church is a second court, with ancient columns, and we had to go through the church itself to reach the cloister, through a door to the left. The fortress walls and this succession of courts gave the feeling that we were approaching some precious sanctuary, and when we reached the cloister we were not disappointed. It is of the twelfth century, and must be one of the oldest in Rome. It, too, has a tended garden and double columns, but, more moving, an utter stillness, like that we felt in the lane at Paestum, where the lizard fell from the wall. Not a sound penetrates from the Vespa-infested streets, and the silence was only broken by a gentle splashing, as a nun watered the garden from a fountain.

Made reflective by this place, after a while we went back into the church, where there are four gilded busts, presumably holding relics of the Four Crowned. The apse is filled with a vast fresco of their martyrdom, but the cosmata floor and the wooden renascence ceiling are more attractive. The ceiling, as rich in carving as those we saw in S. Clemente and many other places, is not, like them, brilliantly coloured and gilded, but left in dark unpolished wood, and shows its essential design in the same way as the brick central *massif* of S. Andrea delle Fratte.

But the Irish boy looked steadily at the four busts, and he seemed to be apprehending the noumena of the martyrs, for soon he said : 'You haven't got to do anything you don't want to. You can always die. There is no MUST. Nowadays we are continually told — you *must* do things that are contrary to your nature and your good feeling.'

He brought out a string of ignominious 'musts', that had been told him at various times. You must choose friends who will be useful to you. You must do work which you believe will be harmful in its final effects, if the rewards are great. You must submit to the destruction of civilized values by the machine. You must not hold back in any way the discoveries of science though they may mean the destruction of humanity. You must not attempt to contract out of the rush of the Gadarene swine to the precipice. These last two are favourite 'musts' of the man with the *New Statesman* in his pocket. So is the one that you must reflect the spirit of your age, even if it means writing gibberish and painting distortion. If you cannot get a good price you must burn tons of wheat, the Corn of Ceres, the Body of Christ, though thousands may be starving on the other side of the world.

There is no *must*, the Irish boy declared. No one has got to do anything that revolts his nature. You can always die. You can be and you must be — this is the only must — like M. Anouilh's ermine which will rather be destroyed by dogs than spoil its beautiful white fur, its *raison d'être*, by crossing the muddy stream. It is that resistance, firm and passive, on which the pure civilization of Turgenev is built.

As for the spirit of our age, every age is doomed. Here in Rome nothing is more evident. What we have to reflect is the Perfect Drawing of ourselves, conceived in the heart of the Supreme Nóos. What distorts that reflection we ignore, even if the dogs get our bodies. He dislikes the bones and relics, but perhaps the bones of the martyrs are different. They are the material substance of which the anguish made those glorious spirits shine.

So here the Irish boy made an advance in his search. He felt his heart illuminated by the discovery that there is no *must*. He had stepped forward into perfect freedom, and this was brought to him by the bones of the martyrs.

CHAPTER IX

S. MARIA SOPRA MINERVA

IT seemed that he was ready to visit churches again, so we went to S. Maria sopra Minerva. As we crossed the wide expanse of marble floor, suddenly, from either side of the high altar, which is the tomb of S. Catherine of Siena, came two single files of Dominicans in their white habits. They stood in the nave facing each other and burst into the *Salve Regina*, singing with vigour and joy. When their song was ended they turned and disappeared the way they had come. It was very dramatic, and gave the Irish boy an immediate feeling for this place, the only Gothic church in Rome.

Although it is not like northern Gothic, nor even as soaring and poetic as that of Tuscany, it is redolent of the Gothic age. The temple of Pallas-Athene, of Hellenic wisdom, is crushed below its foundations. A little to the left of S. Catherine's tomb is that of Fra Angelico, and on it someone has thrown a handful of flowers. Between them is a statue of Christ by Michelangelo, in which he tried to combine the two Stories, for he made him naked, incarnate in his innocence and per-fection. The Gothic noumena could not endure it, and have fitted the statue with a bronze loin-cloth, defiling the Second Adam with the shame of the first. Here, too, is the chapel of S. Thomas Aquinas, the massive foundation of the Gothic structure, the theocratic social system. In Filipino Lippi's frescoes a Dominican has his foot on a prostrate heretic.

But it is the influence of S. Catherine that is most potent here. This is a church of the Dominicans, 'the hounds of the Lord', and S. Catherine was a Dominican tertiary. On our way from Paestum to S. Margherita-Ligure, where, rather oddly, the Irish boy ended his search, we had to pass through the Middle Ages, and we made our first contact here, under these pointed arches. It is usual to think of the north, which gave us the pointed arch, as more fresh and simple and pure than the Catholic pagan south, from which Protestant land-owners imagine, or used to imagine, came all that was evil ; making these statements in the Palladian dining-rooms or picture-galleries of their country houses, where every evidence of the civilization around them came from Italy, without which they would still be dressed in skins with cow's horns on their heads.

And is the north so innocent ? Is not the 'sweet cruelty' more connected with the pointed arch, the piercing spires reaching away from this earth in aspirations which distort our natural lives ? Is it not this soaring spirit that corresponds with 'the anti-human side of a religion that should have been full of love and mercy'?[1] The round arches of the south enclose and protect our human lives, and keep us in scale with our surroundings. The Sainte-Chapelle in Paris, perhaps the most absolute and beautiful expression of the Gothic spirit in the whole world, was built to house a relic of Christ's torture. The beauty of its pointed arches pierces the heart, and it is a place where men might want to go to die in an ecstasy of anguish, to press thorns into their own breasts, rather than to live happily praising God in his natural creation, illuminated by the innocence of his Son.

These ecstasies were frequent in the life of S. Catherine. She was born on Lady Day, 1347, a twin daughter of a wool-dyer of Siena, of whose enormous family only thirteen reached maturity. When she was six years old she had a vision of Christ, wearing the triple crown of the popes. When she was seven she prayed the Blessed Virgin that she might be the bride of Christ. She went into a deserted room and beat herself with a whip. She practised other austerities and

[1] *Turgenev*, David Magarshack.

acts of piety, which, like many of the activities of childhood, were half-serious and half a game. When, to please her sister, she made small concessions to fashion she accused herself with bitter tears of having fallen into sin. When her confessor told her that it was right and not blameworthy to love and please her sister she accused him of failing in his duty. It seems to us that she leapt from the cradle straight into the arms of the devil of the Third Temptation.

She refused to marry to benefit her family, and so was despised by her brothers and made to do all the drudgery of the house ; but at last they were so impressed by her patience that she was allowed to have her own way. She beat herself with chains till she bled, returning to Christ blood for the blood he had shed.[1]

'It is revolting!' exclaimed the Irish boy. 'What is against nature is against God, who saw his work was good. I expect we can't escape suffering. It will come with our effort to straighten ourselves in a distorted world. The wounds we receive are the work of the evil noumena, our enemies. The soldier does not begin gashing himself before going into battle. I suppose the wretched girl was a victim of S. Paul, who is responsible for these perversions, killing Christ as soon as he mentioned him and boasting only in his Cross, which was inevitable but incidental, owing to the rage of Caliban. Why didn't he boast of his innocence, his beauty, his kindness, his devastating wit, his love of flowers and children and good wine, the wonderful art of his parables, his perfection of humanity ? He did not tell S. Mary Magdalene, let alone a young girl, to go and beat herself with chains till she bled.'

We agreed with this, but there were other considerations. We had to consider the time when S. Catherine lived—the age of the pointed arch. There were no anaesthetics and no contraceptives. Man's experience of life was absolute. He knew every pang of birth and of death. He paid to the full for

---

[1] *S. Catherine of Siena*, Sigrid Undset.

everything he got. The great art which we admire was achieved at this cost. It was created by the heart as well as the head, and by hearts that had not shied away from any passion. Looking at their work, our anaestheticized hearts have twinges of life for which their sufferings paid. In the time of S. Catherine the old gods, redeemed or not, had been killed by the invading Goths, or poisoned by contact with Byzantium. Their sweet reasonableness and their serene light had gone. Apollo was buried at Veii, or lying in the mud of the Tiber. There was no classic proportion to check fantastic extremes, and men adored instruments of torture in the piercing beauty of the Sainte-Chapelle.

The awareness of a destiny is at first groping and confused. It makes false starts, and in youth is impatient for the time of its fulfilment to arrive, and so indulges in travesties of its future achievement. S. Catherine felt, but did not know intellectually, that she was to save Rome and the Christian Church, and her strong spirit in the body of an unknown girl could only find expression in beating that body. From the world around her, the world of violence, she saw that nothing could be achieved without the extremes of experience, which is another name for suffering; and so, with youthful anxiety to begin her mission, she inflicted it on herself. Also, though this idea was disagreeable to the Irish boy, since her vision at six years old she had overflowed with love for Christ, and seeing the object of her love mostly in his torments, it was intolerable to her not to share them.

'Yes, but what good did it do?' asked the Irish boy.

Possibly they consumed every part of her that could not be used in her mission, so that she burned like a flame. The reports of her sanctity spread over Italy, not because of the bloody chains, but because of her wisdom which so curiously accompanied them. She brought peace between ancient enemies. She settled disputes between the warring Italian states. Young men and women were so drawn by her

H

character that they became her 'sons and daughters' and acted as her secretaries, writing the replies which she dictated, sometimes three at a time, to the numerous people who wrote asking for her advice and help. She could not write herself, but signed her letters : 'Dolce Gesù, Gesù Amore'.

The popes for long had been in the 'Babylonian Captivity' at Avignon, mostly Frenchmen and largely in the power of the King of France. They appointed French cardinals, and the papacy was in danger of becoming a local institution. They sent rapacious legates to draw off the wealth from their Italian territories. Rome was in a state of chaos. Pilgrims were attacked by robbers, and even wild beasts that haunted the ruins. The popes had degenerated from the splendid stature of Innocent III into self-indulgent French princes, living in an extravagant and often debauched court.

Gregory IX was a Frenchman, pious and anxious to behave responsibly, but vacillating. Catherine wrote him many letters, urging him to return to Rome. At last she went to fetch him, but she was also sent by the rulers of Florence to beg him to remove the interdict on their republic, so great was the confidence of worldly men in her spiritual power.

She set out with two or three of her 'children'. She had no money, her body was weak from her austerities, and she often lost her physical sensibility, lying in a coma while her spirit was in ecstasy. At the papal court one of the ladies stuck a needle into her foot, to see if her trance was genuine. She survived worse tests than this—all the hostility of the luxurious papal entourage, who were afraid of being removed to the stern duties of Rome ; but she so impressed those who mattered, chiefly Gregory himself, that, a few days after she had begun her journey back to Siena on foot, he ended his captivity, returned to Rome, and so saved the papacy. It was one of the most magnificent achievements of the Middle Ages, that this woman without money, without any means of transport, but whose soul burned in her wretched body, could,

like Pius XII nearly six hundred years later, with words alone
— 'potente, serene illuminatrice' — save Rome from extreme
ruin. The noumena were more powerful than matter.

Gregory died soon after his return, and Urban VI was
elected. He not only had to restore order in his own state,
but to resist the claims of a rival schismatic pope. In all this,
Catherine was the dynamic force behind him. She came to
live here, near S. Maria sopra Minerva, close to where we
were now sitting in the afternoon sun, on the steps of the
church. Yet she was not only a kind of celestial fury. She
marvelled at the exquisite perfection of created things ; and
on the Christmas before her death she sent Urban five candied
oranges, covered in gold leaf, which she had herself prepared.
Towards the end she suffered various agonies of flesh and spirit,
and for two days she was entirely possessed by evil noumena,
the devils of the Third Temptation, which had pestered her all
her life. For what child, who at the age of seven demands to
be the bride of Christ, can be endowed with normal humility ?
At last the devils left her, her torments were over, and having
completed the same number of years on earth as her heavenly
spouse, she cried : 'Blood! Blood!' and commending her soul
to the Father in the same words as his own, she gave up the ghost.

Her body is buried here under the high altar, but her head
was cut off and sent in a reliquary to Siena, where it was
welcomed with joyful demonstrations by the crowd, which
included Lapa Benincassa, her mother.[1]

To the Irish boy it was all barbaric and sublime. Yet if
she had not held her body in such cruel contempt, and fought
it relentlessly, would her spirit have burned in a flame so
powerfully bright that it glowed across Europe, and saved
the heart of its civilization ? We cannot judge the people of
another century, any more than we can judge with complete
understanding the art created by alien noumena. We are like
the man with the *New Statesman* standing before the 'Madonna

[1] *S. Catherine of Siena*, Sigrid Undset.

della Serpe'. And anyhow who are we to judge those who led the heroic life, the life without anaesthetics, above all the fragile penniless woman who set out on foot for Avignon, indifferent to the menace of robbers and storms and stony paths, when, if we want to make the same journey, we complain of a stuffy night in the train ?

The Irish boy did not speak for a while. Then he saw a girl riding past on the back of a Vespa, and she turned her head towards us. 'I've seen that girl before somewhere,' he said.

We told him that it was on the ceiling of the Sistine Chapel, and that hers was the face of the Delphic Sibyl.

Behind the wall against which we sat lay the body of the woman whose life was a miracle, and there, according to the legend, Galileo declared : 'Eppure si muove'. There, flowers are thrown on the tomb of Beato Angelico, and there is the chapel of the architect of the never-built City of God on earth. Round the corner to our right is the superb dome of the Roman Pantheon, now a Christian church, and there someone has thrown flowers on the tomb of Raphael ; not as a studied, cultured gesture, but with love. Opposite us Bernini's little elephant looked round with surprise at the Egyptian obelisk which someone had stuck on his back, and that, too, is surmounted by the Cross. A few yards along the steps on which we were sitting, the inevitable *putti*, without whom all this sun-drenched history would be incomplete, with shouts and splendid gestures were pursuing the drama of their gambling game, with the metal tops of mineral-water bottles, as they had no *dieci lire*.

The Irish boy leaned his head back against the wall and closed his eyes, as he loved Italy beyond expression.

★

The next afternoon, on our way back from the Aventine hill, where we had been to S. Sabina, in whose garden S. Dominic planted the orange trees which he first brought to Italy, the Irish boy suggested that we should again go to S. Maria sopra Minerva. He had not yet learned that it is often unwise to try to repeat an experience. We went there and sat again on the steps, where the *putti* were still gambling, but today with *dieci lire*.

The Irish boy asked what Galileo had to do with this church. He had come to a stiffer hurdle than that of S. Paul, though erected by him. There was no way round it so we stated the facts.

Galileo was tried by the Inquisition for heresy in that near-by building which is now a government office, and was found guilty. He was made to recant under threat of torture, though it was not intended that it should be carried out. He was both the protégé of Cardinal Bellarmine and a friend of the pope, but even the latter was unable to stop the processes of the Inquisition. Many people were dressed in fantastic robes and led from this church to be burnt to death. Blasphemous monks held the crucifix to the victims' lips as the brushwood was kindled. So kneeling in this church Galileo denied what he had discovered, that the earth moves round the sun. It was said that when he rose to his feet he said : 'Eppure si muove' — all the same, it moves. This story is now denied, as that kind of witty reckless heroism is no longer admired. It is individualistic. Even if the story is not true, it is in keeping with his character. He was sentenced to what is now called 'house arrest' in countries where political heretics are imprisoned, killed, or tortured. He had to say daily the seven penitential psalms.

The Irish boy's eyes blazed and he leapt to his feet. 'God !' he exclaimed, 'I'd like to burn the bloody place down. Those monks singing to the Virgin in their white robes. They ought to have "We are murderers" printed on them in the colour of flames.'

We pointed out that these were not the same monks who tried Galileo.

'They are not ashamed of what their order has done.   If they were, they'd show some sign of penitence, a large blood-red spot on their habits.'

We asked if he would also burn the tombs of S. Catherine and Beato Angelico, who were Dominicans, and the Christ of Michelangelo.   Good and evil were terribly confused.   If it were not so, his search would be unnecessary.   If he was to find the Nóos amongst the beliefs of the people of his own kind, the people of Europe, he must separate the accretions from the original story.   We saw at Quo Vadis Domine that the evil noumena, enraged at the appearance of the Second Adam, at once began the process of concealing it behind distortions.   S. Paul covered it with his peculiar varnish, to which the foul accretions of the ages have so easily stuck, particularly the grime of Inquisition smoke.   He was not pro-tected, like the other apostles, by three years of contact with Wisdom and Love in the flesh, not like S. James who denied that God tempted men, and defined 'true religion and unde-filed' in one perfect sentence.   But the evil noumena saw their danger from S. Paul's fiery spirit, and so confused his Christianity with a fury of contentious theology, with modes of thought which are nowhere in the gospels.   If Christ had known them to be necessary why did he not lay down clearly in half an hour all the doctrines about justification and faith and grace and predestination and prevent his so-called fol-lowers from burning each other?   But he only gave us the Perfect Mirror in which to adjust our crooked drawing.

The Irish boy had to overcome this obstacle of 'sweet cruelty' of the hellish wickedness of holding the crucifix to the lips of the man you are torturing to death.   To do this we had to glance at the history of Christian persecution.   It began in its punitive form, not with the Church, but with the state. From the beginning the princes have been the enemies of the Church, never more so than when they were corrupting it with nominal support, as in England today.   When the

Emperor Theodosius finally established Christianity, he instituted punishments for those who did not accept the Nicene Creed. When, in A.D. 385, Priscillian, a Spanish heretic, was put to death by the Emperor Maximus, there was general consternation ; S. Ambrose and S. Martin forcibly attacked the Spanish bishops who secured his condemnation. This is the first hint we have of the successive evils fastening themselves on the Church, so that they have become almost the chief marks of 'Catholicism', the 'sweet cruelty' emanating from Spain, the only country of the Christian Mediterranean to adopt the pointed arch. S. John Chrysostom said that to put a heretic to death would be to introduce on earth 'an inexpiable crime'. Pedro II of Aragon in A.D. 1197 was the first to decree the burning of heretics. Up to A.D. 1200 it was the state and the mob, not the Church, which led people to the stake.

Innocent III spent ten years trying to convert the Albigenses, before in A.D. 1208 he allowed punitive measures to be taken against them, and then chiefly because they were a menace to the social structure. When the measures began he tried again and again to stop the savagery of Simon de Montfort. Yet in our Whig histories the popes are villains and Montfort a hero. Clement V, against his will but under threat from the French king, for the first time in the Church's history, admitted evidence secured by torture. At last, in A.D. 1233, Gregory IX instituted the Inquisition with the Dominicans, and with the Spaniard Torquemada, the hell-hound of the Lord. The Church had introduced on earth the inexpiable crime, and had created the confusion which is the constant aim of the evil noumena. Bernard of Clairvaux, author of hymns to Incarnate Love, like S. Paul hounded out heretics, and forging the signatures of the Archbishops of Sens and Rheims, wrote to Rome slandering Abélard, whose intelligence was offensive to his bigotry.[1] The confusion is summed up

[1] Héloïse, Enid MacLeod (Chatto & Windus).

by Voltaire with terrible irony in the sentence : 'Candide was
flogged to the music of the most beautiful plainsong'.

The Irish boy was conducting his search within the limits
of European belief, and although for the moment it is using
methods we had intended to preclude, which have little to do
with the heart and the eye, and which again may bring on
us the charge of amateur theology, we had to glance at the
medieval conception of the Church's place in the world, of
which even the tourist should have a sketchy idea. It was the
conception of a theocentric and theocratic society, one both
centred on and ruled by God, in which the spiritual authority
of the Church was above that of the state. The first unit was
the family, of which the Holy Family at Bethlehem was the
symbol. It was both a natural and a spiritual unit. The local
seigneur or squire was the father of the village ; the king the
father of his people ; and above all was the pope, the spiritual
father of the whole known world. It was a magnificent conception, and if it could have been made to function would have
brought the Kingdom of God on earth. But it was too good
to be worked by fallen men.

There is a hymn which states : 'Like a mighty army
moves the Church of God'. It does not. It is not a single-
minded body full of righteousness. If it is an army, half its
personnel is in the pay of the enemy ; but it is more like a
tree, pushing upwards, through weeds and brambles, choked
by brushwood, sapped by mistletoe, eaten by caterpillars,
sprayed with poisonous chemicals, some of its branches rotten,
others blown away by storms, but with its roots deep in the
good earth, and where it has reached up through the jungle,
the most marvellous flowers, expanding in the Light from
Heaven.

Dom Gregory Dix, an Anglican Benedictine, who spoke
of 'the terrible disintegration of the last 500 years', is said to
have believed that there had never been a true Catholic Church,
that it is like those who compose it, only 'a sketch drawn by

night of its true self'. M. Maritain writes : 'The truth about the world and the earthly city is that they are the kingdom at once of man, of God and of the devil'.[1] The Church, amongst those savage princes, had to secure temporal power to enforce its spiritual authority, and so corrupted itself, and 'men have long remembered the shadow and shiver of this error'.[2]

All the same, under Innocent III the theocratic society nearly became a reality. Innocent achieved, six centuries earlier, what the blundering Protestant democracies which have dismembered the Church are struggling for in godless impotence, the united states of Europe; but Innocent was not only a man of great political strength and wisdom, uncorrupted by power; one who remembered all the time that he wanted temporal rule; not, even so, that the popes might preserve the independence of their spiritual authority and should not, like Innocent IV, have to flee to Lyons because Rome seethed with the Emperor's troops, but that, through that rule, there might come about a transmutation of society, causing it to glimmer with the Light to which the early Church sang as it emerged from the catacombs. When S. Francis appeared before him, asking permission to live in the almost anarchical poverty which is enjoined in the gospels, and the prelates of his court tried to suppress what they thought would be a threat to the structure he was trying to build, he listened to the Cardinal di S. Paolo who said : 'If we reject the request of this poor man . . . shall we not affirm that the Gospel is impracticable, and so blaspheme Christ its author ?'[3] And he gave S. Francis his blessing.

The persecution of heretics, horrible as it was, was at first more the political punishment of those who were trying to disrupt the state than a Pauline delivering unto Satan for theological deviation ; and for this reason it was carried out more violently by the state, especially as the princes seized

[1] *The True Humanism*, Jacques Maritain.   [2] *Ibid.*
[3] *S. Francis of Assisi,* the Abbé Englebert, tr. Edward Hutton (Burns, Oates & Washbourne).

the properties of the murdered men. In the same way in our own time, but without the pastoral anxiety, the restraining humanity of Innocent, Bernard Shaw complacently envisaged the killing of people who would not conform to the machinery of the Socialist state : W. H. Auden, the popular poet, wrote of 'the necessary murder' ; while in Russia, where alone the Inquisition survives, with more devilish tortures, the destruction not only of the body, but with enforced madness and the destruction of the soul, this is done.

However, it is useless and mischievous to bandy atrocities — the Church against the state or Belsen against Hiroshima, and to claim that one side is more virtuous because it has not sunk to the same exact level of hellish wickedness as the other. The object of these reflections was simply to emphasize that because the Church, struggling towards the Light above the iungle, is disfigured by its surroundings, that is no reason for the brambles and the parasites and the diseased growths which have infected it to condemn it as more deformed and cruel than themselves. It is true that the face of religion has been made hideous by the smile of 'sweet cruelty', but it is the cruelty of the human race, which can only be redeemed by the Perfect Drawing.

In the language of the Story, it is the savagery of man to man that causes the blood to flow from the wounds of Christ, and until it stops we cannot remove the crucifix. And we cannot stop it in the world we know. This is not to say that we should not try with all our strength, but if we think that we can staunch it entirely, we shall become like the architect of the medieval theocratic state ; or the democratic advocates of the unconditional surrender of a totalitarian state ; or the fiendish advocates of a racially pure state ; or the architects of the Russian communist state, only lighting the fires of new inquisitions, with the rows of noughts multiplied beyond the power of human imagination. It is the politicians, and they alone, who strew the world with corpses, and when the

Church becomes political it cannot help adding its quota to the carnage.

We left S. Maria sopra Minerva, a little subdued by the shadow and the shiver of those pointed arches. But the *putti* on the steps were shaking their *dieci lire* in their hands, using them as dice-boxes, and they dispelled the ghosts of this place. They at least are loved by the Supreme Nóos. Their noumena behold his Face.

CHAPTER X

A WALK ROUND ROME

THE Irish boy is an extrovert, of healthy instincts, fond of amusement, with no desire to immolate either himself or anyone else on behalf of the unknown, especially of a sadistic theologian's conception of the unknown ; but he is prepared if necessary to make sacrifices on behalf of his fellow human beings, and even to be butchered rather than jump into the mud. He is convinced that beyond this material world are powerful forces, good and evil, which can give him strength for these actions and inactions, can mould him towards a likeness of the Perfect Drawing, or destroy him. He thinks that to ignore them in conceit of the very limited knowledge that even the greatest scientists can achieve would be unintelligent — though he accepts the final statement of the greatest scientist of our time that 'man's chief need is to reconcile himself with God'.[1] Being Irish, of a warm and generous temperament, sometimes the beauty of the world created by the Supreme Nóos, either directly or through the agency of man, fills him, as on the steps of S. Maria sopra Minerva, with great emotion.

He thinks that a mistake of official religion is to present young men like himself with language which can only be used without humbug by extreme ascetics. He does not ask to tread 'a steep and rugged pathway' and he is not acquainted with anyone who does. He much prefers to walk in the green pastures. He is not going to pray for affliction in his sparkling youth, but for the abundant life intended for him by the Supreme Nóos at the Creation, and promised by his Son, who turned the water into good wine.

[1] Einstein.

116

He wanted to avoid for a few days the disturbing reflections aroused by the pointed arch, and to walk about Rome
looking at the people, who live unquestioningly in their
story; the Leonardo faces and the Bronzinos, the seraphic
pieces of life and the tumbling jewels, and the older people
with their aplomb and their expressive gestures. Few of these
are beautiful, and we asked the friend who told us about the
racing motorists, what happened to all the Leonardo faces
when they grew older.

'They lose their beauty at twenty-five,' he said. 'They go
to bed still beautiful on the eve of their twenty-fifth birthday,
and wake up in the morning middle-aged.'

We began our excursions at the top of the Spanish Steps,
where two soldiers were trying to attract the notice of two
girls, who walked quickly on. The soldiers expostulated and
pleaded, with that deprecating plaintive note which is often
heard in Italian voices. The etiquette is that the young man
may be as importunate as he likes, and the girl is safe so long
as she ignores him, treating him like the wind or rain, as an
impersonal force of nature, which perhaps he is. But if once
she notices his existence and replies to him, she is considered
fair game. These two girls did not reply, but they hurried up
the steps of SS. Trinità dei Monti to take refuge. The soldiers
followed them, and the Irish boy was so full of curiosity as
to what was happening in the church that we followed the
soldiers. The girls were sitting together in a pew, and the
soldiers were kneeling beside them, motionless, absorbed in
prayer.

Although intending to avoid for a few days all sights
with theological implications, we have immediately come on
one. In Catholic countries where the noumena are so close to
the phenomena, the former are apt to become involved in
the latter's more dubious activities. But we did not know the
full intentions of the two soldiers. At the worst they must
have been more innocent than those of the two monks who

prayed all night in the little chapel which we are shown at
Blois, for the successful assassination of the duc de Guise ; or
than certain prayers issued by Anglican bishops which we considered a week or so later at Assisi. It seems true that 'religion
penetrating all relations in life means a constant blending of
the spheres of holy and profane thought'.

We left the church, hoping that all would be for the best
between the soldiers and the girls, and went down the steps
past Keats's house. Here, from some hellish sweet-cruel motive,
his friend Joseph Severn refused to let him have laudanum in
his last agony. Then sixty years later he had his old insignifi-
cant body inserted into the same grave as Endymion, as if in
death they were not divided. The twin bay trees are inter-
twined above them near the pyramid of Cestius. On their
equal tombstones are a lyre and a palette. Surely in 1879,
when Severn died, the disparity of their achievements must
have been obvious ?

It was not this that brought the English bishops to our
minds, but the chaste white spire of the red-brick Anglican
chapel, rising modestly in the Via Babuino amidst all the domes
of *Roma Barocca*. On the steps of this chapel a number of
putti, just released from school, were having a scrimmage,
hilariously clouting each other on the heads with their satchels.
The blows had little effect on the apparently tough Italian
skulls, until one of the *putti* banged his head on the red-brick
Protestant wall. He gave a savage biff to the tumbling jewel
he thought responsible, and walked away, both of them looking offended. In a minute he returned and explained to the
other that he had made him bang his head. They had a
reasonable, objective, and rather plaintive discussion of the
situation. Was this contemptible ? Should the one who
received the blow immediately have retaliated, as a manly
boy would have been expected to do in our youth, and the
battle only concluded when exhausted, streaming with blood,
they were separated by their friends ? Could not a commis-

sion of theologians be appointed to decide how much violence it is necessary to inculcate in the young to keep the race virile ? Or has S. Thomas Aquinas already done this and no one takes any notice ?

In the Via Condotti other *putti* returning from school were playing hide-and-seek in the doorways of the smart shops. We could not imagine this in Bond Street, but one of the attractions of Rome is that domestic life permeates the whole city. There are not in the real Rome, the Rome within the walls, special areas for business, for shopping, and for theatres ; though there is that godless tract to the north-east of the Via Vittorio Veneto (itself lined by tourists at café tables, like expensive unsuitable flowers edging a *nouveau-riche* drive), where almost the only church is the Cappuccini, with its crypts decorated like a series of boudoirs, the rococo designs made with the skulls and bones of dead monks.

Near here two youths were staring into an archway with fascinated intensity, hypnotized as rabbits by a snake. The object of their attention turned out to be a girl in tight tartan trousers, with rat's-tail hair, and liver-coloured mouth and finger-nails. Women in trousers are rare in Rome. One of the youths gave the Irish boy a questioning, deprecating, anguished smile, either because he could not understand such a desecration of female beauty, or because it made an unfair and overwhelming appeal to his passions.

We walked down into the old town and it began to rain. We took refuge in a little baroque church near the Campo Marzo. A boy was standing near a stand of lighted candles, fiddling with the wax. When other children came in he seized them and whispered in their ears. They passed on, disappearing through one of those mysterious doors. Two little girls dashed in, flicked the holy water, and danced up the aisle, playing that game of avoiding the joins in the paving-stones, which psychologists tell us is the sign of some deep-rooted fear or perversion. But apparently Italians, not being descended from puritans, have little use for psychologists, though there are a few Viennese importations. As the little girls passed the high altar, they combined, in one lovely flying movement, their leap from the last stone with a genuflexion.

One of those men, now about forty, who had lost his beauty on his twenty-fifth birthday, his face puckered with distress, came in and stroked with supplication the foot of a statue of the Virgin. A brisk-looking business man stood a few yards away and said some prayers. So all day in these plentiful churches of Rome, there are one or two or half a dozen people living in the Story, in contact with the noumena. It is paganism, say the Protestants, with the candles, the genuflexions, the images.

'Great God!' said the Irish boy, 'I'd rather be a pagan, than occupied in pulling down redundant churches.'

The rain stopped and we went on through the Piazza Navona, that great open space, an arena under the emperors, where later carnivals were staged. There used to be a painting of one in the National Gallery, but it has been taken down. This piazza is now a kind of play-pen and day nursery for the children of Rome. Its evocative background, the domes of S. Agnese (not fuori le Mura), the two Bernini fountains, and the playing *putti*, make it seem the very heart of Rome.

In the Vicolo del Curato we were again reminded of Wordsworth. A woman was out walking with her five children and carrying a baby in her arms. It was evident that the family was soon to be increased. The eldest child, a girl of nine, was expostulating with a bent old man at the fecundity of nature, and they were arguing about the size of the family. The mother and the old man were amused. Only the little girl was indignant, as she still replied, pointing with a dramatic gesture at her mother's too fruitful body : 'We are seven.'

We went across the Corso Vittorio Emanuele, where, at

the height of the afternoon traffic, a waiter in a white coat —
carrying, poised high on one hand, a tray with a coffee-pot
and two cups — was threading his way through the motor-
cars and the whizzing Vespas.

At last, strolling without direction, we found ourselves outside S. Francesca Romana, looking down across the Forum to
the Capitolino hill. A large, new, very square and expensive-
looking motor-car drove up to the side door. A priest in
a surplice and white stole came out, and we thought that there
was going to be a wedding, but he had only come to bless the
new motor-car. Certainly all things should be put under the
protection of the holy angels, but will they really protect this
enormous glistening beetle?

We are inclined to believe that the internal-combustion
engine is the invention of evil noumena. It drowns the sound
of the human voice and of the life-giving fountains. If our
civilization is destroyed, this engine will be necessary to its
destruction. If theologians are to discover how much violence
is to be encouraged in the young, they might also discover
how much noise is compatible with the Christian religion.
The loudest noise conceived in the mind of the Supreme Nóos
is thunder. How moderate, innocent, and kind to our ears
this — which seemed the wrath of God to man while he still
lived in proportion to his surroundings — has become to us
who are used to immeasurable violence, rows of noughts in
sound.

We imagine that, in the language of the Story, the natural
world is under the husbandry of God the Father. We are to
co-operate with it to produce our means of life. To violate it
is an act of blasphemy — to blow up an island, destroying all
its natural life, the innocent birds and animals, and to poison
the fish in the sea, simply to satisfy a vicious curiosity as to
how it will be possible to destroy in the same way our fellow
humans.

The priest blessing the motor-car is trying to apply the

I

Story to new developments, but should he bless something which is going to add to the lurking death and the din in the streets of Rome ? In silence we noted, as the train drew out of Paestum, the spirit reawakens and becomes responsive to the natural world and attentive to its meaning.

CHAPTER XI

S. PIETRO: THE THIRD FACE

At last we felt that we were ready to visit S. Peter's, the climax of Catholic power. We crossed the Tiber by the Ponte S. Angelo, flanked by Bernini's angels, and passed beneath the ramparts from where Benvenuto Cellini, so he said, shot the Constable of Bourbon, who led the most monstrous attack the princes had ever made on the Church; and half his army came from Spain; it also contained Lutherans. For three days the centre of civilization was submitted to a rape by this 'Christian' horde which exceeded anything done by the Goths and Vandals and Normans in the past. The Lutherans taught the Spaniards how to spoil and loot the accumulated treasures of the churches, and to violate nuns in the street. Convents were stormed and women flung from the windows, and in those three days Rome suffered a greater blow to its fabric than England in all the years of Cromwell's tyranny, and, like England, one from which it has never recovered. Though in England the injury was also to the human soul of the people.

In eighteenth-century prints we see ornate coaches approaching S. Peter's over what look like the mounds of a rubbish dump, but the modern Via di Conciliazione is not supposed by aesthetes to be an improvement. The great piazza, enclosed by Bernini's columns and brilliant with his fountains, was full of a crowd streaming towards Maderna's palatial façade as we were going to a Canonization Mass, celebrated by Pius XII himself. For fear of being accused of Protestant prejudice, we quote a Catholic writer on this

church, one who states that it was built 'at the cost not only
of the destruction of the most venerable church in Christendom, but of a divided Europe ; for it was the sale of indulgences to build the new S. Peter's . . . that caused the great
scandal which gave life and some excuse to the Reformation'.[1]
It was the church built by Constantine over the tomb of the
chief of the apostles that was pulled down to make way for
this ecclesiastical Versailles.

We have come a long way from S. Giorgio in Velabro
and the faithful emerging from the catacombs to sing their
hymns to the Light. Inside, the place does not quite convey
its vast size because, oddly enough, everything is in proportion.
If those mammoth *putti* on the holy water stoups were the
size of natural children we should realize more easily the
enormity of the building.

Away up beyond Bernini's baldachino were festoons and
festoons of glittering drawing-room chandeliers. The acres
of marble pavement were crowded as for a race-meeting, and
the music of Palestrina fought feebly against the hum of voices
and the shuffling of feet. Two papal courtiers, looking very
like two English country squires, though dressed in red brocade
and ruffles, walked, quietly chatting, up and down the side
aisle, past the Stuart monument. Women were trying to see
the Pope by using their face mirrors as periscopes. Yet there
was a feeling that something was about to happen, an approaching climax. Now, in a few moments the Light of Light will
descend from the realms of endless day, the bread of Ceres will
become the Body of Christ, and the race-meeting will be on
its knees, adoring the Mystery.

Was this an image of the Catholicism envisaged by Dom
Gregory Dix, the Perfect Drawing of the Christian Faith ?
The Irish boy seemed sceptical, but we pointed out that Christ
fed the five thousand by the Sea of Galilee, and doubtless they
gossiped and shuffled their feet in his presence.

[1] *Rome*, Edward Hutton (Methuen).

When the mass was over, the Pope, preceded by the Swiss Guards in Michelangelo's stripes, was carried in his chair down through the crowd to the west door. The Irish boy, who had been told preposterous stories about Roman Catholics worshipping the Pope, expected the whole crowd to fall grovelling, their heads to the ground like Mohammedans at the call of the *muezzin*. But the first sign of his approach was a distant sound of clapping, which grew louder as the chair was borne into the nave. Women waved their handkerchiefs and cried : 'Papa ! Papa !' A group of young Americans called : 'We want Poppa !' The enthusiasm became tremendous when the Pope was carried past, smiling with infinite paternal kindness, waving his gentle hands and blessing his children, the Pastor Angelicus, the monarch who rules as a father. 'Oh, those hands!' exclaimed an Anglo-Catholic standing near us in ecstasy. The Irish boy became so excited that he too called : 'Papa ! Papa !' and one of those hands waved in his direction.

The combination of superlative grandeur and intense humanity in this scene, the gentle radiance of its central figure, had moved him deeply. When that hand of blessing waved towards him, perhaps he was touched by the Catholic noumena, for this experience was almost immediately followed by an advance in his search.

In the treasury of S. Peter's, amongst all the renascence jewels, and the chasubles stiff with gold, he found the Third Face, that of the Christ of Michelangelo's *Pietà*, which we had not seen. It is placed too high in its chapel at the right of the entrance door, but was here revealed in a photograph on the souvenir stall.

The Apollo of Veii showed him animal well-being, which is the necessary foundation of life. The Apollo of Tevere showed him serenity of mind ; but until now he had been unable to find the Face of incarnate innocence, of redeeming love, which superimposed on the others completes the Perfect

Drawing. He has only seen the tortured face on the Cross, the awful bleeding figure, a defeated man conceived by morbid and ignoble men. The early pictures of Christ were of his youthful beauty, Apollo redeemed contained within himself, the rays shining from his head, so that he was praised as the Light, and we still call him : 'Sun of my soul', 'My Star, my Sun', and sing :

> God is their sun whose tender beams
> Diffuse eternal day.

He was not even shown with a beard until the fourth century. Irenaeus, Justinian, and Tertullian, fed on medicated honey, say that he was weak and ugly ; but how could this be true of the revelation of perfection, who 'grew in stature and wisdom, and in favour with God and man', which could only be said of a boy of remarkable beauty ? S. Jerome and S. Basil say that he was beautiful. If it were not so the Incarnation would have no meaning.

To some, this language may seem unsuitable, but one of our aims is to see the created world as it was conceived in the mind of the Father ; or, if that is too presumptuous, as it was seen by Traherne — the young men sparkling angels, the girls seraphic pieces of life. For this we must have the freedom of language used in the great humanist periods, not that of nineteenth-century convention. We do not speak or think of Christ in his boyhood as a sort of satisfactory school prefect, industrious and possibly as good-looking as it is wholesome for a boy to be ; but as sparkling in his beauty, ravishing as the sun, incarnate love in whom we adore all creation ; because not only the tainted soul but the ills and deformities of the flesh came with the Fall, and he had to restore to our sight the vision of all perfection. He is God from the cradle. If he is not born God, the Second Adam, he has not much meaning, only that of another moral teacher, of whom there is an abundance.

THE THIRD FACE. The Christ of Michelangelo's Pietà

S. Pietro

Cold on his cradle the dewdrops are shining,
Low lies his head with the beasts of the stall :
Angels adore him in slumber reclining,
Maker and Monarch and Saviour of all.

It is this we seek at Bethlehem ; not an infant moral prodigy to fatigue us ; but a Jewel of Perfection to inflame our hearts.

It is true that this too is the face of a dead Christ, but it is not a face disfigured and defeated by death, and he might easily be asleep. It is not a face that we pity as that of a little, weak, ugly, tortured man, but worship as that of the unconquered Prince of Heaven. It is the face of the man who turned water into good wine; who with tolerant indulgence forgave the harlot; who told wise ironic parables; who did not think God's high priest worth answering; but blessed the *putti*, and told the thief he would be that night in Paradise. It is the face which stupid and perverted men, lost to the devils of the Third Temptation and cowards in the face of beauty, have tried to show as their own, the hideous victim, the blackmailing governess, but which has here escaped. It is the face of the ermine, slightly disdainful, which would not jump into the mud and so has been slain. Yet it is infinitely kind. It is the kingly head of Gerhardt's hymn :

Can death thy bloom deflower ?
O countenance whose splendour
The hosts of heaven adore.

Here is the Perfect Drawing, the beauty long desired ; and yet it not only resembles, but has something of the same expression as the little boy who was thrown again and again into the sea at Amalfi.

★

Perhaps as we left S. Peter's the Irish boy was in a state of hubris, asking for the inevitable check. In the great atrium he saw something which had escaped his notice as we entered with the crowd.

'What are these hideous white-marble slabs ?' he asked.

They were those that record the names of the bishops who were present at the promulgation by the Pope of the dogma of the Assumption.

'What was that ?' he asked.

That the body of the Blessed Virgin did not see corruption but was assumed into Heaven has long been a pious belief, though not accepted by everyone. S. Thomas Aquinas is said to have questioned it. But within the last few years this promulgation has made it compulsory for the faithful, and necessary to salvation.

'Did S. Thomas Aquinas then, after seven centuries in heaven, plunge suddenly into hell ?' asked the Irish boy.

We pointed out that in theological matters one cannot be exact. Nothing alive is exact, only the dead things. No trees — although their perfect drawing, the tree conceived by the Creative Nóos, may have a mathematical symmetry — on this earth no more than ourselves exactly reflect their conception. Again only the limited mind can be exact. The great truths have to be symbolized in the Story.

'Then why make exact definitions about them ?' asked the Irish boy. We explained that this definition was an addition to the Story. 'It's not in the Bible,' he said.

The Church's authority, we believed, was above that of the Bible, even that of the gospels. Christ gave his authority to the apostles who had known him, without any qualification that it was to be subject to books written a hundred years later, and certainly not to the Old Testament, which he had superseded. That was the beginning of the Church, the company of those who had lived with Perfection in the flesh, before any gospels or epistles were written ; those who had heard all the things he said which were unrecorded, and of which the whole world would not contain the volume. That was the Church of the pure honey. Since then it has taken the evangelists and made them symbols in the Story — the

Lion, the Book, the Eagle, and the Bull. Because of this it does not matter if there are discrepancies in the gospels. The Story itself is in the guardianship of the Church.

If the Church is to live it is essential that it should be above the Bible. Christ is not only a historic figure, imperfectly recorded. He is also an object of intuitive apprehension, and it is in this second capacity that he is most alive, above and independent of his moment of revelation, existing through all time — the Logos in the beginning. And he is more clearly apprehended by the artist and the saint than by the theologian, giving an impossible task to his limited intellect. There is more truth about the Incarnation in the Madonna della Serpe, painted by the blackguard Caravaggio, than in all the suffocating glut of commentaries on the Pauline epistles. But the artist and the saint alone cannot be certain of the truth of their apprehensions. They may only be valid for themselves. The Church must purify them in the light of its wisdom ; and it must be above the Bible to clean the Face of Christ, to remove the varnish and all its accretions. The intuitive artist provides it with the materials.

'But this legend of the Assumption is another accretion,' said the Irish boy. 'It doesn't purify anything and it has no meaning, not in the way the essential Story has meaning. How could the body of the Blessed Virgin be received into heaven? Where is heaven ?'

We thought that heaven was a spiritual region where the good noumena had power.

'Then how could the *body* of the Virgin be there ?'

We pointed out that if he was speaking as a Protestant, it was not more impossible than that the Body of Christ should be there. We do not know how the Catholic authorities regard the story, but we feel that it must be much as we do. The Pope who promulgated this dogma has recently (forgetting, it seems, the Tower of Babel) given an approving audience to the Space Travel Society, which would be

incompatible with a physical interpretation of the dogma.
The Church has outpaced Galileo. As to meaning, is not
the Blessed Virgin perhaps Ceres redeemed, the Mother who
produces the corn and wine become the Mother who produced
the Body and Blood of Christ, and therefore should have her
place in heaven ? This dogma may be needed at this time,
when every effort is being made to mechanize man himself,
so that following mechanized nature he, too, becomes dumb
— to ignore the claims of his humanity ; when the talk is not
of men but of manpower, a word no Christian can use. This
reminds him that his destination is heaven.

'It ought not to need so much explanation,' said the Irish
boy. 'It's a deliberately placed stumbling-block.'

We had to admit that it has this aspect, and that on the
whole it was unfortunate. We had met Catholics in Rome
who, as a result of it, said they would never go to church
again. At the time of the promulgation many people, dis-
illusioned by the war, revolted by man's inhumanity when he
had discarded Christian sanctions, were turning to the Catholic
Church as the only hope for the world and civilization, and
this seemed a deliberate slap in the face for them. We cannot
know who was responsible for it, but it would not be the
Pope alone. It is said that the Dominicans, perhaps partly
with regard to their greatest member, S. Thomas Aquinas,
strongly opposed it ; but the Jesuits are the most powerful
order in the Church. Their Superior-General, 'the Black
Pope', is the only man who can enter the Pope's apartments
at any time he chooses. Spain, which had given the Church
the hounds of the Lord, also has given it the soldiers of the
Lord. But Christ did not call his apostles dogs and soldiers,
but shepherds. The Jesuit order, founded by a soldier, using
military methods, appears to think that the Church should be
run like an army, strong through discipline, with redeeming
love merely a sop to make it tolerable. Clement XIV sup-
pressed them, was poisoned, and died in agony. When after

forty years they were reinstated, immediately they sprang up like swords from the ground, their organization and their serried ranks complete. They have brought thousands into the Church but they have also kept thousands out. They are believed by Protestants to keep the mentality of the rack and the stake, and to say to the convert : 'Admit you're wrong. Admit you've never been right. Admit your sacraments were a silly game. Lick the dust. Sign, damn you, sign on the dotted line. Admit we control the Holy Ghost. All right, bring in the thumbscrews.' We feel this is a wildly exaggerated picture ; but Cardinal Newman described the Ultramontanes as 'an aggressive and insolent faction', and it is possible that they thought this dogma would make the converts grovel more abjectly, would force them to a more complete abjuration of their reason, and prevent any access of liberalism or elasticity to the Church. For the military mind can only think in terms of discipline and defeat, not of redemption.

Even so, amongst the Jesuits themselves there are signs of reaction against this attitude. It is said that in France some of their younger priests have stated that 'the saints of yesterday taught above all how to free oneself from created things. The saints of tomorrow will teach us how to use them. . . . Sanctity is the presence of God in a man whose gifts have not been mortified or sacrificed, but have been harmoniously developed to the highest level.' This seems consistent with the direction of our search.

It would be a tragedy for all of us who hope for the survival of civilization, if the Ultramontanes, thinking to create loyal Catholics by destroying their intelligence, made the structure of the Church so rigid that, like a house which never sways a little in the wind, it were to collapse when the storm comes. The Catholic's brittle mode of thought does not allow this possibility, but we who are a kind of fellow travellers on our pilgrimage, may recognize the danger.

But, of course, it could not entirely collapse. Whatever the hierarchy say, the woman at Amalfi will still teach her baby to wave to the Virgin ; the shopkeeper will still put his bowl of incense in the street, and fling down the flowers before the Bread of his body and soul ; and the dumb boy will still touch the cross of the dying thief.

These considerations were accompanied by a terrific clanging of bells from the top of Maderna's façade, declaring with joy that five new saints were round the throne of God. Opposite where we sat at the edge of Bernini's circle of giant columns, his fountains flung their dazzling spray against the purple noon. Beside us the little horses waited patiently in their red-wheeled carriages. We realized that we had fallen into the sin of Cerebration, instead of living happily in the Story, and, like those smashing bells, rejoicing that the saints were in heaven, and that we were sitting in the sunlight of Italy.

*

To purge ourselves of our sin we risked our lives twice a day with the frustrated racing motorists, and spent the rest of the week at Fregene, worshipping the Dionysus of Maccarese and the Ephebe of Subiaco. The following Sunday was our last in Rome, as we did not intend to penetrate into the baroque of the Counter Reform. We think it is architecturally great fun, but its exuberance is not the life we seek. The spirit does not shine for us through all that swirling flesh. We even resent it for the sake of the serene life that it has destroyed or smothered.

We had another reason for not conducting our search in that region. The Irish boy was brought up in the English Church which separated from Rome before the Counter Reform. His search is only amongst his spiritual antecedents. The Roman Church itself was tainted by the Reformation, as we always are tainted by what we violently oppose. After a

war against National Socialism we became National Social-
ists. The Roman Church, since we left it, has acquired things
that are not in our spiritual ancestry ; it has given a further
bitter taste, a taste of iron to the already medicated Pauline
honey. It may say : 'Come to your true mother', but it is
not the mother we left.

On our last Sunday we went to S. Anselmo on the Aventine
hill to hear the mass sung by the Benedictines. It is a little
disappointing that plainsong, older than the Christian Faith,
is sung by its masters, both here and at Solesmes, in new
buildings. If this mass were celebrated, say, in S. Giorgio in
Velabro or in that old church of the time of Charlemagne
above the hill at Châtillon, the effect would be overwhelming.
Even here in this new building with its polished marble, it is
deeply impressive.

There are no shuffling crowds, no pushing tourists, no
putti squabbling on the altar steps. The congregation is
attentive and silent, except when singing the alternate clauses
of the Creed to a melody from remote antiquity. The cere-
mony is slow and ordered and the Story is presented in its
grave beauty. An African, black but comely, stands near the
Abbot holding a light in one of those flat candlesticks with
which we went to bed as children. Is he bringing back to its
source the Light sent out to lighten the Gentiles ? Clement,
John, and Paul, Cosmas and Damian, in whose houses we
have been, are named as the Light approaches, and through
them we enter the heart of the Story. After the Communion
a young man returning from the altar appears serene and
illuminated. He feels perhaps that the imperfect sketch of
his nature has been straightened. The Nóos who conceived
his true self has entered him, and while he retains the aware-
ness of this he will be full of strength and gentleness, and know
all that he ought to do.

That was our last visit in Rome, the best picture that the
Irish boy could take away with him, except that on the

following day we went again to the Piazza di S. Pietro, where at noon the Pope gave his daily blessing to the city and to the world. When he appeared at his window in the Vatican he was greeted with that gentle clapping, not loud in the vast space, but like laughing water, mingling with the sound of the fountains. The paternal hands waved in blessing. The Anglo-Catholic was kneeling on the stones crossing himself. The Italian women waved their handkerchiefs. The Irish boy smiled and said : 'Papa ! Papa !' We hoped that we had received some virtue to help us on our search.

CHAPTER XII

TODI: THE POINTED ARCH

IN the afternoon we left for Terni, and there changed into a
little train belonging to a private company, which squealed
pompously up through lovely fertile valleys to Todi. Everywhere in Italy is humanity, human kindness, and human
passion, and that sort of humanity which seems to give meaning to the routine of ordinary life. In a country train or a
country bus where everyone has preserved his identity, where
life is still in scale with nature, it is strongest. Above all it
is strongest in a Catholic country, where the family is the
reflection of the Madonna and Child. So in the crowded
little train they all chatted together.

There are two railway stations for Todi, and we were told
that, coming from Terni, we should alight at the second. At
the first we saw the town far above us, and wondered how the
train could possibly climb that height in so short a distance.
From the second station it was still as remote, looking mystical
in the evening light, a shrine of the Holy Grail. We were
disconcerted, wondering if we were expected to climb some
steep and rugged pathway to those celestial ramparts, but
fortunately there is a bus service.

In the morning it was clean and cold in the Gothic town,
though it was midsummer. There were no tourists and we
were the only sign of the existence of foreign countries. We
were in a different atmosphere from the south, due not only
to the higher altitude and lower temperature. 'It is always
cold in Todi', said the chambermaid. We felt alien, in spite
of the friendly country people. The peasants, as they must
have done in the Middle Ages, have brought in their produce,

great piles of glowing fruit from their farms without the walls, to sell in the arcaded market-place. For here the antiquity is purely medieval, not rooted in Greece or classical Rome. Because it has not been 'done over' with renascence or baroque, the effect of antiquity is almost greater than in, say, S. Maria Maggiore, which, though more distant in time, is closer in spirit to ourselves. Also Rome is the centre of our civilization, the spiritual capital of every civilized European whatever his belief; and so there we are all, in a sense, at home. Other parts of Italy, however beautiful they may be and however friendly the people, are more a foreign country to us. But the fundamental change of temperature, physical and spiritual, is due to our having entered the region of the pointed arch, of aspiration and anguish.

We found them immediately in the church of S. Fortunato, the first Gothic church we entered since we began our search, excepting S. Maria sopra Minerva. Here under the high altar is buried Jacopone di Todi, who in 1279 lost his wife and became a Franciscan. He is the mystic who gave to Italian poetry its sharpest note of religious experience : 'vissuta nelle sue accese esaltazioni . . . e nelle sue tormentose nostalgie del divino'.[1] Here it all is — the aspiration and the anguish, the sharp note, the exaltation, the tormented nostalgia for the life beyond this earth. He is believed to have written the *Stabat Mater Dolorosa*, the poem which for seven centuries has been the supreme expression of the sorrows of womanhood.

We decided at Paestum that the noumena we were seeking were those which are the source of all beauty and goodness and abundant life, which would enable the Irish boy to live in harmony with them and with the natural world. When he has found them he will be faithful to them, to death if necessary, like the ermine ; but he will not from sheer morbidity press thorns into his flesh. Yet it is true that the grief-stricken mother stood at the foot of the Cross, and has stood there

---

[1] *Enciclopedia Italiana.*

through all the centuries since. The Irish boy felt detached
from it, but not necessarily hostile. He felt that the *Stabat
Mater* was a beautiful hymn, yet again there comes that note
which he distrusts, 'the sharp and piercing sword' — the
pointed arch.

In a chapel down the church we saw some tricolour flags.
In Catholic churches all the evidence, even if we do not care
for some of its expressions, is of devotion to God and his
saints. Nothing else is allowed room, and certainly not pro-
minence. At any rate this is so in Italy, though in France we
have seen an image of 'Our Lady of Armies' standing on a
trophy of cannon balls and bristling swords ; while S. Joan of
Arc is rather more prominent than the Mother of Christ, as if
the purpose of the Incarnation was to free France from the
English in the fifteenth century. In English churches memorials to soldiers are more conspicuous than those to the saints,
and a visitor from another planet might imagine that God's
purpose was to establish the British Empire in the nineteenth
century. So far in Italy we had been free from this mis-
interpretation, and we approached the chapel with misgiving.
Would we find there some boasting inscriptions, implying
that the victims were fortunate in their end, such as the
wicked Old Testament text on the machine-gun memorial
at Hyde Park Corner, or something like the bombing
planes in the stained glass of Ely Cathedral ? We read the
commemoration :

'Quanti essi soffrirono, quanti agonizzarono sui campi di
battaglia. . . . Accettate il sacrificio che essi fecero della
propria vita, le lagrime di tante madri, di tante spose, di tanti
poveri orfanelli chi inconsolabili ne piangono la perdita.'

Here, a few yards from the tomb of Jacopone, the mournful mothers are weeping. The deep humanity of the Italian
heart could tolerate no humbug, and faced the stark reality of
its tragedy, the rows of noughts who suffered, 'quanti agonizzarono', the mothers and the young wives and the poor

K

orphans, who in our own country are kept well in the background, while the soldiers themselves are only allowed a platitude. This extreme of vulgarity, an insensibility to others' anguish, which perhaps at first an affectation, from long use becomes a reality, we call good breeding.

Yet is it right that young people should be forced too soon to contemplate tragedy ? They will find enough before their lives are over, even without wars. It is healthy that they should turn away from the dark and tortured images and turn towards life, towards the Light and try to be the Ephebe of Subiaco redeemed. So while admiring the honesty of this memorial, which faced the reality of its subject, we passed on, feeling that the widows and weeping orphans were, and we hoped could remain, outside the scope of the Irish boy's search.

But it so happens that as we are writing this chapter, the news has come of the martyrdom of Hungary. There, almost with their bare hands, boys and girls younger than our Irish companion are attacking the murderous tanks, come again to crush the reviving human spirit. Thousands of children, rows of noughts, are sent over the frontier to safety, possessing nothing but their names pinned on their coats. What can console them, who have faced tragedy before their time ? A statue of the noblest youth, the most shining Apollo, would leave them indifferent ; and even a picture of the Holy Family would remind them of what they have lost. Only the *Mater Dolorosa* is enough, whose tears mingle with their own, and her Son on the Cross, whose blood mingles with that of the brothers they have left behind.

However, we had come to Todi not to see the little Gothic city, beautiful as it is with its cathedral and palaces, but the Tempio della Consolazione, built by Cola di Caprarola and possibly Bramante, on a spur of the hills outside the walls. La Consolazione is the flat contradiction of all that we have seen in the town. It would have to be outside the walls, forced there by the spirit of Jacopone, as S. Paolo is excluded by the noumena of Rome. Here there is no sharp note, no 'tormentose nostalgie del divino'. This building is the expression of pure logic. All is sweet reason. It should give its misleading name to the church which shelters Jacopone, and call itself 'Tempio di Santa Ragione'. Consolation is within the walls, under the pointed arches — at any rate the consolation of the heart, though here there may be other consolations. The four half-domes support the square, and from the square rises the great central dome, round and accepting the limits of the mind ; not reaching upwards in the uncontrolled longing of an ever-diminishing spire, ending in a point, in nothing. Most satisfying, it looks exactly the same from every side, which we expect of reason.

Inside it is as perfect as without. There is no ornament beyond the logical division of the pilasters, and the splendid carvings of the symbols of the evangelists in the four spandrils supporting the dome. But do the evangelists support anything so logical ?

When we left Todi this was the image we took away, not of weeping orphans but of the triumph of reason, standing boldly on its hill without the walls and declaring the noble principles of the human mind to the Umbrian valley.

Yet it is reason alone, in the urbane Pilates uninfluenced by any divine nostalgias, which has caused so many mothers to stand at the foot of the Cross.

CHAPTER XIII

ASSISI—S. FRANCIS AND THE CROSS

TODI was a kind of lock, necessary between Rome and Assisi, where we changed the level of our search. At La Consolazione we said good-bye to reason, to the Second Face, to the serene adequacy of the human mind, and in S. Fortunato we became aware of the nostalgia for a different serenity, one that could only be reached beyond and above the anguish of the pointed arch.

We went on by the private railway to Perugia, where we only stayed an hour or two, as the Irish boy was impatient to reach Assisi, which we could see from the ramparts. It was flung like a handful of silver on the slopes of Monte Subasio, twenty miles away, and it appeared half miraculous, bathed in celestial light, the Bethlehem of the West, heightening those vague, ill-informed and beautiful ideas which the Irish boy had about it.

In 1939, at the apex of Fascist power, S. Francis, the apostle of humanity and non-violence, was named with S. Catherine co-patron of Italy. As the Irish boy was conducting his search in Italy, he thought he should pay attention to those whom she considers her greatest saints. He had given a very brief glance at S. Catherine, whom he could not help admiring, but felt that her life could hardly be an example for his own. On the other hand, he was predisposed towards S. Francis, as he had heard that he was the man whose imperfect sketch was adjusted most nearly to the Perfect Drawing. He also knew that he had a great love of nature, composing hymns to the sun and to all creation, and in this combined the Greek and the Christian stories. He therefore felt that when he came

to that little city, shining on the hill-side, he would experience
a similar illumination ;   not an external light shed on him as a
natural phenomenon, but illumination from within.

Our arrival in the late afternoon at Assisi satisfied all the
Irish boy's ignorant and beautiful preconceptions.   We went
down to S. Francesco, into the upper church.   From the darkness at the far end came a sudden burst of singing, of strong
young voices declaring to the same ancient melody we heard
at Amalfi, the melody which haunts the Catholic churches of
the whole world :

> Et antiquum documentum
> Novo cedat ritui.

The effect was as dramatic as when the Dominicans
streamed out from behind the tomb of S. Catherine.   Moving
up the church, we could see the source of this robust music,
about fifty monks and novices occupying the stalls of the
basilica.   Their attitudes were free and different.   Their praying
faces or their bowed heads, revealed by the light of candles
from the altar in the transept, suggested an illumination in a
missal.   When the service was over they flocked out of the
church, unregimented but reverent, without any affectation
of solemnity to cover uncertainty of belief.   The setting sun
came through the apse windows ;   so on the faces of these
young monks sweeping past was reflected a light which the
Irish boy thought came from within, though the light was
reflected equally from the long expanse of Giotto's frescoes,
glowing down the nave.

We dined on the terrace of the hotel, and the sky above us
was full of birds.   The waiter said that it was always so, and
implied that their presence had something to do with S.
Francis.   We agreed with reverent scepticism, but the Irish
boy, who was always anxious to make the romantic appear
rational, in other words to combine the two Stories, said :

'It may be so.   The animals are obedient to the Creative
Nóos.   When they come into contact with a saint who obeys

the same law, though in a higher octave, they recognize a member of their own obedience and have no fear of him. If in S. Francis they found someone who had towards them the benevolence of their Creator, their descendants might instinctively remain in the place where this happened.'

Early next morning, as at Amalfi, there fell into the silence the note of a deep-toned bell, but the development was different. It began a tentative broken rhythm, sometimes struck softly, sometimes louder, as if itself were awakening. Then behind this sound and woven into it, other bells began a curious melody, perhaps older than the *Pange Lingua* or the plainsong of S. Anselmo, so remote that it might really be sounding from *une cathédrale engloutie*. It did not, as at Amalfi, call to arms, but to redemption.

As soon as we were ready we went again to S. Francesco, which, while we were in Assisi, drew us daily like a magnet. In the lower church, embowered in its wide vaults, the frescoes of Giotto and Cimabue tell the gospel story. The noumena speed across the inky sky to succour dying love. This church is richer, darker, more mysterious than the one above, as if it were the roots from which the upper church springs. And this, in fact, is so, for not only does it provide the material foundation, but the story which it records in confused legend and symbol, springs into clear historic light in the church above, into a new story in which the old is repeated in simple terms. As the first story found its interpreters in the four evangelists, so this later story found here its perfect interpreter in Giotto. At least that is what the Irish boy had been led to believe, and these frescoes — so delightful in themselves, so innocent in their drawing and in their limpid colours, still bright after seven hundred years — confirm his beautiful and uninformed ideas. Here S. Francis is preaching to the birds, and here Innocent III is dreaming that he will support the toppling Church. It all seemed like a vision of Paradise, compared with which those of Beato Angelico are sophisticated.

In the afternoon we had tea in the piazza opposite that temple of Minerva with its chipped and blackened columns, which was Goethe's first glimpse of the classical world, and to which he hurried, ignoring Giotto and Cimabue. To us, fresh from Paestum and the Diocletian baths, these few dusty pillars did not convey much classic sunlight. We found more light in the clean grey-gold stones of the basilicas, and in the clear loveliness of the frescoes. The Irish boy was near to accepting the pointed arch.

The next morning we saw from the hotel window two large bunches of flowers, whizzing down the street apparently of their own volition. As they receded we saw that they concealed a boy on a bicycle. An hour or so later we saw them again, on either side of the tomb of S. Francis, below the lower basilica, where a nuptial mass was being said. We waited discreetly by the stairs, but about a dozen tourists in charge of a monk came down and stood behind the wedding guests. While the priest at the altar was beginning the Canon, the monk in a rather louder voice explained the points of interest to the tourists. The shock which this irreverence gave to the Irish boy was quickly followed by another. On returning to the lower church, we were taken into a sacristy to see some relics of S. Francis, amongst them his habit, like a piece of old sacking — a patched, poor, and dreadful garment for a human body, which, according to Blake, is the phenomenon of love :

> For Mercy has a human heart,
> Pity, a human face ;
> And Love, the human form divine,
> And Peace, the human dress.

The Irish boy stared at it for a while, and then said : 'But Christ had a seamless garment, too beautiful to be divided'.

The incident of the tourists and the sight of these rags had disturbed his poetic and inaccurate ideas about the saint, and it seemed now to be the time to correct them. He was, for the moment, put off more sightseeing of this kind, and we climbed up and sat on the open grass hill above the town, beneath the old castle walls. Here, looking down on the scene where was acted the drama of the man who most nearly reflected the Perfect Drawing, we briefly considered his life, as we had glanced at that of S. Catherine on the steps of S. Maria sopra Minerva.

S. Francis was born about a hundred years earlier. If we like we can go down there and throw some lire into the room where he was born. Her father was a dyer, his a rich and socially ambitious cloth merchant, who gave him all the money he needed to enable him to associate with the young nobles. They liked his reckless liveliness, but probably he was sometimes made to feel, by the inevitable boors amongst them, that he was of an inferior caste, which perhaps gave him his sympathy for the 'under-privileged' ; though he had the chief aristocratic trait of complete indifference to public opinion. Richly caparisoned, he went off to join the army of Walter de Brienne, but seeing a poor knight in the company, he gave him his entire equipment. His father gave him a new outfit, but he only reached Spoleto, and there decided not to go to the war after all, and came home. Various clerical lives of S. Francis state that he received 'hard blows' from God ; but all that happened was that the spirit of innocence in him revolted against the brutal vulgarity of so much human activity.

He loved banquets and fun and dressing-up, but then found these extravagances unbearable when the destitute were sleeping in doorways. As he was a lively and passionate young man, he indulged, according to Thomas of Celano, in other debaucheries ; and when we read that in later life he had to fling himself among thorns or into the snow to curb his desires, it seems very likely. Again clerical biographers, with their sex-obsession derived from S. Paul, and not from the fresh air of the gospels, write : 'We cannot think that he ever strayed from purity'. Why not, if they can complacently accept that he went out to knock Perugians on the head ? As we shall see later, to certain 'Christian' minds the most sense-less butchery is more harmless than a little youthful friskiness.

S. Francis at least could understand the comparative importance of the three temptations, and his lifelong struggle, like that of S. Catherine, was against the devils of the Third. Whatever his lusts, his love remained innocent, and what the clergy like to describe as the hard blows of a schoolmaster God, were really the checks which his innocent but untried love received when he made experiments to express it in wrong directions.

He did not come up against God — unless God is the schoolmaster invented by the theologians, the savage beast who demanded the blood of his perfect Son — but against the evil in his own fallen nature or in the world around him. That was the cause of his pain, his innocent impulse frustrated by evil. The greatest theological lie, the one that more than any other is likely to send the Irish boy back to Paestum, is that evil, misfortune, and cruelty can proceed from God, who is the sum of all good, revealed in his Son, who on this earth did nothing but good, shedding pleasure and kindness and healing wherever he went ; so that, as we saw in 'L' Ultima Cena', the youth who still is nature's priest sleeps close to him, while all around the theologians argue. And it was the sleepy boy who the next day was the only one of them to stand at the foot of the Cross.

S. Francis laid a magnificent banquet and then took out the food to the poor. He flung his whole purse full of gold into the shrine of S. Peter. With doubtful honesty he sold some of his father's cloth to repair a chapel. All the time we feel that he was as much concerned to get rid of his possessions as to relieve the poor. But after he had flung away his own or his father's riches there was always more, and he realized that the only thing to do was to renounce his father, even returning

¹ less harmful

his clothes, which he did formally in the presence of the Bishop of Assisi, who sheltered his nakedness with his cope, as we see in the frescoes. It appears that what S. Francis wanted to do was to live in innocence and love ; which, if he had only known it, or perhaps he did, is the greatest of all luxuries, and one for which the highest price is demanded.

He 'above all execrated money, and both by word and example urged his brethren to flee from it as from the devil'.[1] The absolute poverty on which he fanatically insisted for himself and his followers, even forbidding them to own breviaries, was essential to the attempt to recover their innocence, to be again in harmony with the natural world. This was why Christ was born in the stable, not because of poverty in a sordid sense, only in that of non-possession. More than this, because he was the Second Adam, born again in innocence, he had to be born amongst the blessed and sinless animals who are still obedient to the Nóos, and follow the simple laws of their unfallen being. Turgenev, after watching the preparation of the guillotine for an execution, said : 'The horses that had drawn the van were the only innocent creatures.' [2]

So, when S. Francis had achieved this state of non-possession he could find the greatest enjoyment in created things, calling them all his brothers, except the ants — for in everything there must be some imperfection — 'whose activity seemed to him too restless, and their planning exaggerated'.[3] He knew that we cannot love God unless we love the whole order of the natural world, for that is what was conceived by the Creative Nóos as the expression of material beauty. He may, like the artist, still be groaning and travailing in his creation, and improving it with the ages. So, as we have seen, Perugino and even wicked Caravaggio had a clearer understanding of God than the theologians who make pre-

[1] *The Mirror of Perfection*, Brother Leo.
[2] *Turgenev*, David Magarshack.
[3] *S. Francis of Assisi*, the Abbé Englebert, tr. Edward Hutton.

sumptuous speculations about what they cannot see. We do not mean those theologians who help us to apply the Story to our daily lives. One of the former came to S. Francis and asked him to explain a passage in Ezekiel about warning the wicked, the favourite pastime of his kind, from S. Paul downwards. S. Francis replied : 'The servant of God ought so to burn and shine in his life . . . as to be a rebuke'. He was hostile to much use of the intellect, from the same motive as his dislike of the ants. The Bishop of Terni, after he had preached in that town, 'declared publicly that God had once more made good come out of evil in bringing forth fruits of salvation by means of a man so poor and miserable, and what was more, had so little intelligence'.[1]

As the Irish boy is conducting his search through the heart and the eye rather than through reason alone, he finds all this sympathetic to him. But he does not want to violate his reason. He thinks the statement : 'Credo quia impossible', merely idiotic. It must be possible to worship his God in La Consolazione di Todi.

We continued the story of S. Francis. In penitence for a natural gesture of repulsion, he kissed a leper. His brethren first lived among and served the lepers. When one of these came to the convent, he shared a dish with him, though the leper's fingers bled into the food. When in Lent he had eaten some cakes with lard in them, he had himself led naked with a rope round his neck into the public square. He seemed to be fond of stripping himself naked, which was perhaps part of his impulse to recover the innocence of nature. When a friar accepted a piece of money, he made him take it in his mouth and place it on a piece of asses' dung. A friar who had spoken angry words ate asses' dung as penance. When he was ill and a friar cooked him a special dish, he poured ashes on it before eating it. He appeared to agree with S. Paul, rather than Blake, that : 'We are made as the filth of the

[1] *S. Francis of Assisi*, the Abbé Englebert, tr. Edward Hutton.

world, and are the off-scouring of all things'. Nor did he
accept Christ's command that when we fast we should have
the good manners to conceal the fact beneath a worldly
appearance. When he found that the brethren at Bologna
had a convent built for them, in his passion for poverty he
turned them all out, including the sick. He ordered some
brethren who were planting out cauliflowers to plant them
with the leaves in the ground and the roots in the air, to test
their obedience. One who refused to do this he expelled
from the Order. He treated his own body savagely, refusing
even necessary covering when he was ill with fever in midwinter, and brought on himself disease and an early death.
'His sickness and poverty', wrote Brother Leo, 'are a mirror
to us in which we may look with pity and see the sickness and
poverty of Our Lord.' ¹

The Irish boy was speechless for a few moments, then he
exploded. 'Christ was never sick,' he declared. 'He was the
Perfect Drawing conceived in the mind of the Absolute Good.
If we want a mirror in which to see his human form divine,
we have a better one in the Apollo of Tevere than in this morbid horror. If we want to return to the innocence of the
natural world we have the Ephebe of Subiaco, and the poor
mutilated Hermes in the Court of the Belvedere. Did Christ
ever turn the sick into the street? When the woman poured
scented ointment on to his feet, did he add some horrible
stink to it and insult her, as Francis insulted his good kind cook?
Would he who loved and understood the natural world and
used it for all his references, have flouted the Creator's laws
with that imbecile order to leave the roots waving helplessly
in the air? I wish I knew where the friar who refused was
buried, I'd go and throw some flowers on his grave. He was
like the ermine. And did Christ injure and destroy his perfect body, the temple of the Holy Ghost? He left it to the
Calibans and the devils to do that. He too was the ermine.

¹ *The Mirror of Perfection*, Brother Leo.

Did he hurt the feelings of his rich hosts by refusing their good food, and did he refuse luxuries to others ? Did he wear squalid and disgusting rags ? He had the fine seamless garment, too good for the soldiers to cut up. How can they call this wretched man the mirror of Christ ?

'We are not made of the filth of this world,' he went on. 'If the Story has any truth we are made in the image of God. The world is full of beautiful men and women and children, the creation of the Supreme Nóos, who saw that they were good. There is no mention anywhere of Francis, like Christ, embracing the *putti*, the lovely children, only the lepers. There are no *putti* anywhere in the whole of those frescoes as there are none in S. Paolo, an extraordinary thing in Italy. They were too busy behaving like children themselves to pay attention to their rivals, the real ones. It is not death and the crown of thorns that have deflowered the kingly Head, the Third Face ; it is the theologians and masochists who for 2,000 years have been occupied in making it unrecognizable, presenting it with the hellish distortions of their evil imaginations. I can understand Goethe preferring the Temple of Minerva.'

The Irish boy was too heated for any further discussion to be useful at the moment, so we followed his suggestion that we should go down to the piazza and have a drink before luncheon. An old man, presumably in emulation of the saint, was feeding pigeons and teaching them to take the seed from his lips. The Irish boy sat where he could not see him.

His anger never lasted for long, and after a glass of wine he seemed complacent enough for us to return to the subject of S. Francis. We pointed out that he was born in a time even more primitive than that of S. Catherine, a time without anaesthetics. Christ lived in a far more civilized period, under the firm rule of the Roman Empire, when people could be influenced by words as effectively as by dramatic gestures. In the time of Francis, Innocent III was striving magnificently to create his theocratic society, but with savage and disorderly material. The heretics, as we have seen, believing life was evil, wanted to destroy the social order. The clergy were largely corrupt, and the heresy was partly due to men naturally refusing to receive the sacraments from drunken and debauched priests. It was in these conditions that S. Francis set out to reaffirm the principles of non-violence and non-possession, which are the basic teachings of Christ. He saw that the Church with all its terrible faults was, as it is today, the only functioning means for the redemption of men ; so he only said of the vicious clergy : 'If they hinder the salvation of the people, vengeance is God's'. He was not intellectual and so was non-political. He tried to teach through the heart and the eye, which are the instruments of our own search. He could not argue about non-possession, he could only live it, and, like S. Catherine, he had to do this in a world so used to extremes of brutality, greed, and lust, that only extremes of renunciation could be noticed.

All activity was extreme. The same people were capable of acts of the vilest cruelty and of lofty chivalry and devotion. There were heights to which we cannot rise today ; and depths to which, outside totalitarian countries, most of us would prefer not to descend. The hideous gargoyle and the pointed arch were in the same building. 'To prevent Christian bloodshed and destruction of the people on which my heart has compassion,' wrote the Duke of Burgundy, even one hundred years later, 'I wish that by my own body this quarrel may be settled, without proceeding by means of wars'; and he challenged Humphrey of Gloucester to a duel. We cannot imagine such a message sent today by an English Prime Minister. 'Philippe de Mézières planned his Order of the Passion to ensure the good of the world. The young King of France will easily be able to conclude peace with Richard of England, young like himself, and also innocent of blood in the past.' Yet in this same noble civilization it was necessary for Boniface VIII to forbid 'the boiling of the bodies of princes who died away from their native land, so that the bones might be more easily extracted and sent home for burial'.[1]   For all through the Middle Ages the papacy tried to exercise this humanizing influence.   In 1139 the Lateran Council forbade the crossbow as too murderous a weapon, and successive popes condemned bull-fights and excommunicated those who took part in them.

At that time each man was immediately responsible for his deeds.   He had to experience all he did in his own flesh.   If he wished to sack a city, he did it at the head of his troops, and saw the burning, the corpses, and the rape, so that finally in horror he might repent.   He had no anaesthetics, whereas the bombing plane or the rocket is itself an anaesthetic to the modern ruler, and even to the modern general.   The cautious and refined methods acceptable, say, in English vicarages, would have been useless amongst such people.   If S. Francis wished to show his compassion for the leper, he had to endure the bleeding fingers in the dish.

He took the ideas of chivalry and stripped them of that violence which ultimately destroyed them.   He also stripped them of their greed, for war was a business for the knight. With a good ransom he could found a noble family.[2]   Instead Francis took Poverty as the lady of his devotion.   He rejected every false standard of his age and tried to restore it to innocence.   If he did it by means which to our age are repulsive, it is unimportant.

'But the way he did it was a form of suicide,' protested the Irish boy.

He had to do it in the only way he understood.   He was not intellectual, nor even particularly intelligent as the Bishop of Terni pointed out ;   but his heart was full of love and compassion for his fellow men, and he could only make the gesture of abandoning everything he had, even health and life itself,

[1]   *The Waning of the Middle Ages*, J. Huizinga (Penguin Books).
[2]   *Ibid.*

in recognition of their suffering. It was a gesture of chivalry, made in an age utterly different from our own, the age of the pointed arch, when rulers offered to fight duels to save their people from suffering and the bodies of dead princes were boiled. The gods of Greece were lost, those noumena of proportion. The Second Face was hidden in the mud of the Tiber, and La Consolazione was not to be built for another 300 years. There was no logic to separate the splendid vision from the gargoyle.

'That is what I object to,' said the Irish boy.

But S. Francis could not help it. He was perhaps unconsciously seeking those older noumena of sunlight and freedom when he flung away his clothes and called the phenomena of nature his brothers. He was a victim of S. Paul, who never glanced at the lilies of the field, and would only boast in the Cross of Christ, not in his living humanity, and could only think in terms of the Old Testament, of the blood sacrifice to the tribal god. S. Francis, unintellectual, had no weapon against this. To express the love bursting in his heart he thought that he must boast in death, until he felt the nails in his own body.

'Of course, if your love is frustrated you want to die,' admitted the Irish boy wisely. 'But you don't want to be morbid.'

It is not morbid to recognize the suffering and tragedy in human life. It is only morbid if you regard its evil as good, if you think the wounds, the disease, and the dirt are sent by God. Perhaps S. Francis did this, but it is hard to see in what other way he could have affected his generation. If he had had the equipment to do it intellectually what might have been the result ? He might have become like Calvin, the lawyer theologian, who respected possessions ; who took even the medicated honey of S. Paul and infused it with bitter hatred ; who, like Torquemada though with less scope, put the 'heretic' to death ; who degraded man's nature to the basest level, and gave birth to all the sterile cruelties of puritanism. What could Giotto have made of the life of Calvin ?

If we see what we most love destroyed, we want to die, too. That was the feeling of S. Francis. Few of us are designed for such expiation ; but it is not always morbid to contemplate the crucifix. As Christ showed us how to live in innocence — to which we have most regard — he also showed us how to die in innocence, like the ermine refusing to plunge into the mud. We have been brought up to see this through a thick varnish of sentimentality, to see the soft-eyed blackmailing governess moaning about sorrow ; to hear the embarrassed voice of an academic vicar reading what he instinctively feels is in bad taste, and trying to produce a note of sympathy. The crucifixion is not a domestic misfortune. It is a stark and splendid tragedy, godlike in every detail. It is only tolerable when it is presented free from any personal interpretation, as when the Passion according to S. John is chanted on Good Friday. Then we see clearly the Third Face stripped of all its morbid veils. It is not that of a meek, sick, poor little man. It is utterly noble and the arrogance is sublime. Even after scourging, wearing the crown of thorns, he gave no answer to Pilate, who warned him : 'Knowest thou not that I have power to crucify thee and power to release thee?' He answered : 'Thou shouldst not have any power against me unless it were given thee from above'. When we hear these words chanted in the hieratical, impersonal, and yet dramatic music of Vittoria, free from the mawkish expression of the parson, the Story becomes incandescent with truth ; for it is eternal and can only be seen clearly when it is formalized above the idiosyncrasies of any one generation. So it goes on to the end. Whatever is done to his body, his words have perfect wisdom, perfect reason, and to the dying thief perfect love. On the Cross we see the most glorious creature the world has ever known, butchered by oafs. The noumena rushing to his aid are thick in the air about him, and because

L

men were as yet too stupid to see the supreme tragedy of the world taking place before their eyes, the noumena, beyond matter but able to control it, blackened the heavens and ripped the veil of the temple apart. The worship of the savage god was ended. Who, seeing and knowing what was done, could do anything but wish to die when Perfection is killed? It is only possible to cry :

> His dying crimson like a robe
> Spreads o'er his body on the tree.
> And I am dead to all the globe,
> And all the globe is dead to me.

For those who are young and strong and look forward to a good life, to feel this once a year is perhaps enough. S. Francis felt it all the time. Because of this he saved the Church in his century, and popes and cardinals protected him as its greatest treasure.

CHAPTER XIV

ASSISI—HOME THOUGHTS FROM
ABROAD

THE Irish boy, having accepted these considerations, was able
to stay in Assisi with more peace of mind. On the next afternoon we went down to S. Damiano. We asked the way of
some workmen sitting at a café table outside the Porta Nuova.
They not only directed us, but watched us to see that we took
the right turning, and when we did not shouted to a peasant
on a bicycle laden with produce to get off and show us the
way.

At S. Damiano we went into the church to see the crucifix
— not the one that spoke here to S. Francis but is now at
S. Chiara — but another, carved in 1637 by Fra Innocenzo da
Palermo, remarkable for its expression of extreme anguish,
the sweet cruelty of the Counter Reform at its height. The
majestic symbol has become as real as a street accident. We
could only glance at this crucifix in its dark side-chapel, as
Benediction had begun. A monk looked up from his prayers
and asked : 'Americani ? Francesi ? Tedeschi ? Inglesi ?'
When we admitted to the last nationality, he stood up, prepared to act as our guide. We left the church and he followed
us, explaining the points of interest. As with Maddalena at
Amalfi, we begged him to return to his devotions, and said
that we would wait for him. He did so, but apparently the
thought of unattended tourists was more than he could bear,
and he came out again while the service was still in progress.
He began to show us round, even leading us through the
church, between the altar and the choir where the monks were
now singing *Tantum Ergo*.

155

Though S. Damiano was restored by S. Francis, it became later the home of S. Clare and her poor nuns. The monk showed us the stalls where they sang their office, pathetic rough boards. Most things that survive from the distant past are those that were well made for the rich, and there was something unusually touching in this simple carpentry ; as also in the remote silver sound of the little bell which the monk rang, which had called the sisters to their prayers 700 years ago.

He showed us the little garden where S. Francis composed his hymn to the sun, and the corner of the dormitory where S. Clare died. Though he could so casually interrupt his prayers, he seemed almost in tears as he showed us this spot, and was disappointed that we were not equally moved. In this room is the window from which S. Clare repelled the Saracen armies which came in from the coast, ravaging the countryside, just as they were about to sack Assisi. She took the Pyx from the chapel and stood with it at this window. The Saracens' horses reared, terrified, and they fled back the way they had come. The monk did not question the truth of this story. The Irish boy thought it might be true, but without a supernatural explanation. In Assisi his responses were inclined to be more cautious than in Rome.

We went to S. Chiara to see the crucifix which spoke to S. Francis. The figure is painted on the cross, and shows Byzantine influence. The stomach protrudes. The face is not tortured, but bland and slightly foolish. The Irish boy did not believe that it could speak to anybody. We suggested that it did not literally speak, but only in the way that there are 'sermons in stones'.

We went down into the crypt to see the tomb of S. Clare. The approach is eerie and we felt oppressed at being in the bowels of the earth. The tomb is beyond a grille, with a light shining on the embalmed body of which the blackened face shows amongst the robes. A nun with a stiff black veil like a mask covering her own face asked the Irish boy : 'Ameri-

cano ? Inglese ? Deutsch ? Francese ? Italiano ? Spa-
gnuolo ?', waiting after each word for his assent. The Irish boy
was so horrified, both at the blackened face of the saint and
the sweet soliciting voice coming from behind the black mask,
that he could not reply. The nun was evidently racking her
brains to think of other nationalities which he might have
and said : 'Argentino ?' but the Irish boy fled for the stairs,
and we followed him up out on to the piazza, where we sat
on a low wall looking over the valley, and he used the same
arguments as at S. Teodoro.

'Why should the bodies of these saints,' he asked, 'which
they did not think worth elementary care when they were
alive, but kept them filthy and diseased, suddenly become
objects of veneration when they have ceased to be potentially
beautiful and are really rubbish ?'

It was unfortunate that in Assisi there were no places where
he could for a day or so escape these problems — no Fregene,
no Borghese Villa, no secluded gardens with trickling fountains. The Franciscan noumena and the pointed arches were
everywhere. He was like a child who could only go on
eating more unwholesome sweets to take away the flavour
of the last one.

We made a slight break by going down to S. Maria degli
Angeli, the great baroque church built to shelter the little
Chapel of the Porziuncola, the first home of the friars, and the
place where S. Francis died. It is dark and hard to see the
frescoes. One might well travel in Italy with an electric torch
as well as a pair of opera-glasses. In the cloisters is the garden
of rose-bushes, descendants of those into which S. Francis
flung himself to punish his lusts. The blooms are flecked with
dark spots, originally caused by his blood. In the passage to
the rose-garden is his statue holding a nest with a white dove,
which we thought was made of china, but it suddenly moved
and turned a beady eye on us, giving for a moment a slightly
miraculous effect. This sort of thing does not worry the Irish

boy, white doves and spotted roses. They are only amusing
embroideries on the Story, a little syrupy to our palates, but
they harm no one, and there is no cruelty in their sweetness.

But the chief magnet in Assisi was the superimposed
basilicas, and every evening we went there to hear the monks
sing as the darkness fell, *Adoro te devote latens*, to the Solesmes
melody. On Sunday we went to the mass in the upper church,
where Giotto's frescoes were alive in the morning light. The
monks filled their stalls in the tribune, and the mass was sung
to the same melody that we heard at S. Anselmo, and have
heard at Solesmes, in England and on the other side of the
world. It would be hard to think of more beautiful conditions
in which to venerate the Redeemed Corn of Ceres.

But tourists strolled in groups about the church. They
even passed between the altar and the congregation. The man
with the *New Statesman* had now appeared in Assisi. He had
been joined by his wife, and they stood near the altar, talking
and pointing up at the frescoes, as if the priests were children
playing a rather silly game. The critic of the *New Statesman*,
who for some reason attended the Queen's coronation, wrote
that 'the Communion Service was frankly a bore', and as this
couple follow the 'line' of their paper far more slavishly than
a Catholic follows his religion, they think this is the correct
cultivated attitude. It is strange, whatever their belief, that
they should find this rite uninteresting, as they would give
the most serious attention and discussion to a wireless pro-
gramme on, say, 'Beetle Worship in Paraguay'. Yet the
origins of this rite are in remote antiquity. The choir answering the priest is the survival of the Greek chorus. The tone
he uses for the *Sursum Corda* has sounded for more than 1,000
years in the churches of Christendom ; and all those churches,
all the countless splendours of their vaults and domes, were
built simply to embower this mystery, in which the groping
symbolism of older times — the sacrifice of the fruits of the
earth, the pantheistic compassion for the suffering of the corn

— breaks through to its true meaning as the sacrifice of the
Perfect Being for our redemption, the descent of the Bread from
Heaven. It is odd that this is boring to the 'educated' mind.

However, most of these people who ignored the Mystery
were not readers of the *New Statesman*. Those had gone down
to the lower church to shed their patronage on Cimabue, and
their place had been taken by a woman who was reading
a guide book, only a yard or two from the altar. For the
minute when, if she believed the Story, the Hosts of Heaven
were spreading their vanguard before the descending Light,
she stopped reading, crossed herself as the bell rang, and then
returned to her book.

A group of tourists was standing before the stalls, looking
up at the monks. One of the latter left his place to speak to
them, we imagined with reproof. On the contrary he was
only offering his services as a guide, and he, too, stood near
the altar on which now lay the Bread from Heaven, and
pointed informatively up at the frescoes.

The Irish boy was bewildered. His belief was still un-
certain, and throughout his pilgrimage he claimed to be a free-
thinker, but he had a profound reverence for the Perfect Being,
and for these sacred rites. Yet these people who behaved
more casually than they would in a cinema are Catholics.
They believe firmly and truly that for which he is still
only groping ; though as his search has proceeded, the first,
idea which he provisionally accepted, that Christ was the revelation of the Nóos, had become more real to him, a kind of incarnation in his mind. He found anything which dishonours
it, like the behaviour of these people, painful and distressing.

When the mass was over we left the church and sat at the
top of the grass slope outside.

'I can't swallow it,' said the Irish boy suddenly, 'the
corpses, the lepers, the ashes on the food. They plug all that
stuff but they don't even believe the Story. If they did, they
couldn't behave like that. S. Francis at any rate execrated

money, and made his followers put it on the asses' dung. What would he say of these people who ignore their God to get 100 lire ? The only function of this place must be to create Protestants.'

He spoke more as if wanting to provoke a convincing reply, than as a final statement.

We suggested that perhaps he was temperamentally a Protestant, or at any rate an Anglican.

'Shall we return to England, then,' he asked, 'and finish the search there ?'

At first it seemed that the Anglican Church might present fewer obstacles. It was separated from the great body of the Catholic Church by a political misfortune, due to the temporal power, but it acquired new virtues. It appealed for its doctrine and practice to the Church as it was when men first sang their hymns to the Light in S. Giorgio in Velabro and in S. Clemente. Although it translated the Old Testament into English, for 300 years it largely avoided the errors resulting from this — the Cromwellian massacres and iconoclasm, and puritan sadism, so that under the Commonwealth a boy could have his ears cut off for whistling on Sunday. It held to the main pattern of the Catholic religion with its orders and sacraments. It produced great divines like Lancelot Andrewes and the Catholic-minded Carolean bishops, and poets like George Herbert and Bishop Ken. Like the Church of Rome, it has had its debased periods and its captivity, but at its best it may have made the closest approach to that ideal of Catholicism to which we have referred. In the early nineteenth century when, equally with the papacy, it was thought to be finished, it had a sudden access of new life. There was a new crop of divines, from Pusey to Bishop Gore. Because of their sound Catholic learning, Cardinal Wiseman longed for them to join and enrich the Roman Church in England. Religious orders were founded again, and Anglican services, after an age of incredible slovenliness, were restored to unique dignity and beauty, with the ancient ceremonies of Sarum. More than all this it produced its saints, men like Father Wainwright and Father Dolling, who penetrated into the vilest forgotten slums — where they were at first stoned — and turned them into the dwellings of happy people. Many years ago we sat one evening in the chapel of an Oxford college, and heard a clergyman of great piety and learning explaining to a small group of undergraduates, with much reference to this region in which we are conducting our search, and to Plotinus and to Fénelon, how serenity might be obtained in the spiritual life. It seemed to us then, sitting amongst these serious youths, that we had reached the plane on which the human heart and mind was most illuminated, and that the English Church was the finest expression of the Christian faith.

'Then let us go home,' said the Irish boy.

First, we must take other considerations into account. The Roman Church now declares the Anglican Church to be not only schismatic, but entirely heretical, deprived of the Holy Ghost, which they say has descended through the hands of their bishops since the apostles. This does not worry us much as we feel that the Holy Ghost, the rushing mighty wind, is disinclined to accept their restrictions, and we incline to the view that 'by their fruits ye shall know them'.

But let us return to what is more within our competence. There is a new obstacle in the Anglican Church, inherent perhaps in its domination by the state, but recently become almost insuperable. It has developed a new story, not like that of S. Francis, a repetition of the first Story in a different key, or like that of the Assumption, an innocent embroidery. On the scarves of its army chaplains is a cross, and above the cross is a crown, but it is not the Crown of Thorns, or a crown of glory, but the Crown of England. We are not at all concerned with politics, but we have to look back to certain events for the light they throw on this.

In the century between 1815 and 1914 England was at

war in sixty-four years, France in fifty-eight, and Germany in ten.[1] The Established Church could not fail to reflect the policy of the state, and so we find the War story, like the Crown above the Cross, has largely dominated the Christian story. In S. Paul's, the only Anglican cathedral built between the Reformation and recent years, there are statues or other memorials of eighteen soldiers, eleven naval officers and other ranks, three artists, two doctors, one judge, one musician, and one clergyman. The pulpit is dedicated to the memory of a captain in the Punjab cavalry. Anyone who came here from a place where the Christian religion is unknown would inevitably infer that its chief activity and virtue was the killing of people of other nations. There is no image of any saint, or memorial, except for the one clergyman, of those whose lives have been devoted first to God. On a plaque to the right of the west door, two soldiers 'agonizzano sul campo di battaglia'. As they close their eyes in their last anguish, they doubtless think that now this hell of hatred is over, and that the Mother of Consolation, who feels the sharp and piercing sword for all who suffer a cruel death, will lead them tenderly into the eternal day which surrounds the Prince of Peace — but no, on the cloud in the heavens where they hoped to see her, is their ubiquitous general with his adjutants.

S. Paul's is the extreme example of this Anglican identity between Christianity and war, but it is evident in every parish church throughout the country, and has grown stronger in the last one hundred years. Charles Kingsley declared that Christ was 'not only the God of peace but of war'. Father Stanton recruited vigorously amongst the young men he had saved for the aggressive and predatory South African war.

In 1914, wrote Mr. Lloyd George, no one, not even the German Emperor, wanted war. 'The nations backed their machines over the precipice.'[2] S. Pius X died of a broken

---

[1] *A Century of War, 1815–1914*, Captain G. de St. C. Stevenson (Rees).
[2] *War Memoirs*, Lloyd George (Nicholson & Watson).

heart. At Christmas 1914 the German soldiers came out of the trenches and said they would not fight again unless the English began. There was nearly a second Incarnation, but the generals forbade it. In 1917 the Catholic and Christian Emperor Carl, like the Duke of Burgundy, to prevent further destruction of the people on whom his heart had compassion, sent offers of peace which only those drunk with sight of power could reject. 'L'empereur Charles veut sincèrement la paix,' wrote Anatole France, 'aussi tout le monde le déteste.' Lloyd George, by now full of the devils of the Second Temptation and Old Testament blood-lust, ranting about 'the sword of the Lord and of Gideon', demanded 'the knock-out blow'. When the war was over the Allies kept up the blockade for six months, and a million Germans died of starvation.

During these activities, the Bishop of London blessed the guns ; and refused ordinands who would not first join the army ; the acolytes in Anglo-Catholic churches wore the khaki livery of Mars, instead of the white livery of Christ; an Anglican clergyman put before Lloyd George the idea of total war, and was rewarded with a bishopric; Archbishop Davidson told us that he wished he was young so that he could go too.

While leading Anglican members of parliament sent a telegram to Lloyd George at Versailles, demanding savage retribution from Germany ; while the Allies occupied their country, and the French forced them to provide brothels of German girls for their black troops, the German youths wandered round in penniless romantic groups, having, they believed, renounced war for ever. In 1930 Stresemann said to Austen Chamberlain : 'If you could have made me one con-cession I could have won the youth of Germany for peace. That you would not or could not is our tragedy and your crime.' The path was clear for Hitler with his devil's religion, the gas-chambers and the concentration camps.

We are not trying in a short space with our limited

knowledge to point to the architects of our ruin, but to see how much the English Church endorsed it, what protest or even moderating influence came from the Anglican bishops. We know of none. When the war was over they blessed memorials all over the countryside, in which there was no mention of the agony of the soldiers, the mournful mothers, and 'i poveri orfanelli chi ne piangono la perdita'. Only the baseless clichés : 'For Freedom', 'For Civilization', with space for the next list of names.

In 1939 Mr. Neville Chamberlain, declaring war, said that we had no quarrel with the German people ; but an Anglican bishop wrote to *The Times* cursing them in violent Old Testament language.

As the war proceeded the bombing massacres of civilians, with whom 'we had no quarrel', became more devastating. 'It is the party spirit,' said Stendhal. 'We commit the greatest cruelties but without cruelty.' An area was encircled with fire-bombs so that no one could escape, and then high explosive was dropped in to stir up the flames. A letter was written to Archbishop Temple asking him to use his influence to check this kind of war. He replied that 'the one thing that is certainly wrong is to fight the war ineffectively', adding 'when it is all over we shall have to find some way of showing justice and mercy'. Three weeks later he attended a meeting in the Albert Hall against gambling. In reply to a further letter he said that 'the Church and State were the same people acting in different capacities'. If the martyrs of the Colosseum had known this, they could have thrown their incense to Caesar for the sake of national unity. He also wrote that what made the blockade in 1919 so wrong 'was not the amount of suffering involved', but the fact that it was illegal. The rows of noughts do not matter. But the death of Socrates, the Crucifixion, the throwing of Christians to the lions were all legal. The intervention of S. Telemachus between the gladiators was illegal. Dr. Temple is now one of the most revered authorities in the English Church. When he died, the *Manchester Guardian* said of him :

One service of outstanding value to the church and nation he certainly rendered during the war years. His plain, direct and sane pronouncements on the subject of pacifism and on the justification of aerial bombardments of military objectives certainly steadied many people, and possibly prevented something like a stampede in the pacifist direction when England's danger became less and advocates of an agreed peace became more vocal.[1]

They did not know that he failed to regard any objective as non-military. So now we may consider some rows of noughts which cannot be dissociated from the Anglican Church ; and perhaps compare them with the feeble achievement of Torquemada, who, in his long life as Inquisitor-General, engaged in the inexpiable crime, reached a total of only 2,000. In Dresden nearly 30,000 people were encircled with flames, battered, and roasted to death in one night. In Würzburg, in March 1945 when the Germans were in their last stage of collapse, on the Feast of the Annunciation of Our Lady, when Redeeming Love entered human flesh, the Allied bombers killed many thousands of people in twenty minutes, for no apparent reason at all. Later, when it was known that the Japanese were seeking peace, the atomic bomb was dropped on Hiroshima ; and a few days afterwards the plutonium bomb, from mere scientific curiosity, was dropped on Nagasaki, with its 60,000 inhabitants, as the pilots could not reach their objective, a town of 240,000. The man who gave this order was granted an honorary degree at Oxford.

★

Here we paused, as the deacon singing the Passion on Good Friday pauses when he has told of Christ's death ; which we also have done, but in our Story Pilate has not washed his

[1] *Manchester Guardian*, 24 October 1944.

hands, paying at least that tribute to virtue.

An Air Force chaplain addressing some pilots engaged on the above-mentioned activities told them what splendid work they were doing. They replied : 'What we do is not Christian, but we are not Christians', and they walked out in contempt. At least they would not lie to the Holy Ghost. If they are in Paradise, saved by this fundamental honesty, what do they think of the bombing planes erected to their memory in the stained glass of Ely Cathedral ?

The reply to our protest may be that it is emotional. Would those who seize on this easy word, if they had to watch their children roasted to death in Dresden, or going blind four years later in Hiroshima, feel no emotion ; and if so would this make them admirable ? In the Story the children of Dresden are our own.

But we should remember that in war we have all done dreadful things, that bishops have little imagination. They are brought up on an island, they are not European-minded, and their brothers are politicians and generals. Most of them have been army officers and have military decorations, or else schoolmasters, trained to administer discipline and punishment rather than pastoral love. It is not in the war-time Church of England that the Irish boy might find his home, but in that Church as it is today.

After all, S. Peter denied Christ, but he afterwards went out into the porch and wept. Has the Anglican hierarchy, waking up in horror, washed its hands ? Has the Archbishop of Canterbury, with abundance of tears, climbed on his knees the steps of some broken altar in Munich ? Have the Anglicans, having collected £1,000,000 to rebuild their one ruined cathedral, sent the money instead to Dresden or Nagasaki or Monte Cassino ? Such an action would have been natural in the time of the Duke of Burgundy and Philippe de Mézières. On the contrary the War story is still imposed on the other, the design on the chaplain's scarves has not been changed.

In 1954 the Church Assembly rejected an amendment condemning the hydrogen bomb and declaring that the Christian faith 'regards the moral law as absolute, and not relative to the needs of the state'.   And so the War story is the reference in nearly every Anglican sermon, as if it were the main instrument for correcting our imperfect drawing.   We hear over and over again as opening sentences from the pulpit, not 'when S. Francis first tended the lepers' or 'when Christ entered Jerusalem' but 'when General Montgomery liberated France'.   We have heard an Anglican bishop say : 'When God planned the Incarnation he was like General Montgomery planning D-Day'.   An Anglican vicar said : 'Field-Marshal Montgomery was a kind of John the Baptist'.   We have heard an Anglican priest in a sermon compare Christ's effect on Jerusalem with that of Mr. Churchill during the Battle of Britain.   We have heard an Anglican bishop quote Mr. Churchill's idea of heaven.   It would be unfair to mention these things if they were isolated instances, but the whole Anglican Church is permeated with military imagery instead of that of the saints, the gospels, and the Company of Heaven.   They use such terms as 'Christian Commandos' and 'Operation Firm Faith'.

In 1955 all this reached its logical conclusion, a step further even than the official denial of the moral supremacy of Christ. The late Archbishop of York gave his approval to the manufacture of the hydrogen bomb, at which a member of the Government exclaimed : 'No one can any longer say that the hungry sheep look up and are not fed'.   The Corn of Ceres, the Bread from Heaven, for the Anglican has become the hydrogen bomb.

After the war, the Archbishop of Canterbury, speaking at the Albert Hall of the foundations of Western culture, said that they were Greek philosophy and Roman law, and that we had 'received from Palestine much else indeed, but at least this, the Sovereignty of God and his moral law'.   This is why we have come to Italy, to seek here the 'much else' which the Anglican Church officially declares only exists as relative to the needs of the state, and seems reluctant to mention.

During these home thoughts from abroad, the Irish boy had become pale and distressed, and finally he put his head on his arms. An enormous wolfhound came over across the grass and sniffed at him sympathetically, and he put out a hand and blessed it unaware. Perhaps it was a descendant of the Wolf of Gubbio. The contact with this kind dog soothed him a little, and he said :

'Well, anyhow, we still have the animals. They only kill when they want to eat, and they never kill their own kind, which alone we call murder ; except the rats, as there is always an exception. They do not think the natural world menacing and hostile. They do no violence to it, but co-operate with it, or they could not survive. It is a lie that nature is savage and bloody. Even the stinging bees co-operate with the blossom on the plum trees, and if they use their stings they die. Only men are savage and bloody, and the clergy are the most bloody of all. They are a hideous black phalanx to hide from us the Face of Christ. The butchering politicians and the bombers will receive the judgment of God, but they will be forgiven. On the clergy will fall the terrible Wrath of the Lamb, which is reserved for those who confuse his teaching, who poison the honey, and cover his face with black varnish.'

We did not think that it would be much use to continue with the subject in his present mood ; to point out that those who drew on themselves his condemnation were men appointed to the House of Lords by the state, or those who hoped to be so appointed ; that there were a far greater number whose lives were given up entirely to doing the greatest good in their power for a wage that an unskilled labourer would despise ; that people in trouble turned first to them and took it for granted that they should help ; and that there was a high proportion of them who felt as much distress and bitterness as the Irish boy himself at the utterances of their superiors ; and that it is possible that, when the Church of England frees itself from the state, it may again become the Church of Andrewes and Ken, Keble and Gore, and fulfil its peculiar function of stating an innocent Catholicism, and forming a bridge over which all Christians may pass to complete reunion.   Their orders have not yet been condemned *ex cathedra* by Rome, or even if they have, while we regard the Pope as the undoubted head of the Christian Church (the Church of England can never be more than the Church of one people) and the Guardian of the Story, we are fairly certain that the Spirit bloweth where it listeth.

It was nearly time to go to lunch, but the Wolf of Gubbio had settled itself comfortably against the Irish boy's back, and he did not like to move for fear of offending it.   To fill in the time we said we thought that the Roman Church was like a cake with good food at the centre, the raisins and the wheat, but covered with elaborate and sometimes shocking icing, coloured here and there with poisonous dyes, and much of it made of plaster of Paris, which could break one's teeth.   The Anglican Church was a cake of more gentlemanly appearance, fit for a general's or a landowner's luncheon table, but one began to suspect that the flour had been sterilized, and that the raisins, rather sour, were from his own kitchen garden.   Also one might break one's teeth on a bullet amongst them.   If you could get through the Roman Catholic icing, which we admitted was too much for ourselves, you could be certain of the good food at the centre.

In the afternoon we went into the shop in the cloisters, where they sell postcards and souvenirs.   The Irish boy bluntly asked one of the monks : 'Why do you allow tourists to walk about between the altar and the congregation at mass?'

The monk's eyes flashed with indignation.   'It is disgrace-

M

ful,' he said. 'It is a terrible example for the novices, but we
are powerless. The whole place belongs to the Government.
We can't even take a photograph of our own church without
a stamped permit from an official in Perugia. It is no different
from the money-changers in the Temple. It is exactly the
same.'

The Irish boy was greatly relieved at this explanation, and
for the rest of the day appeared so contented that we did not
like to point out that it was unlikely that the officials in
Perugia compelled the monks to leave their prayers to act as
guides.

In the evening we went for the last time to Benediction at
S. Francesco. The Host was brought to the high altar of the
upper church, where a smart woman stood chatting brightly
to two men, beside a notice marked 'Silenzio'. A long double
row of monks in surplices, each carrying a candle, formed for
a procession down to the lower church. They began to sing
the hymn to the Glorious Body, in the melody now so familiar
to us. In the lower basilica they knelt in a large square round
the altar. Their lighted candles threw up a soft glow on to
the splendid colours of Cimabue's vault, as they sang the
Tantum Ergo. Two men pushed aside the monks kneeling at
the corner, to get to the other way out.

'Perhaps it would be better here in the winter,' said the
Irish boy a little wistfully, as we walked back up the hill.
'There would be no tourists. Imagine those monks kneeling
there in a pool of light in the dark empty church, and outside
the fields and the silent streets covered with snow. It would
really be like Bethlehem.'

When we drove away in the morning this was the picture
of Assisi we took with us, not as we had really seen it, but as it
would be in the winter, when in undisturbed devotion the
monks regained the strength to endure the summer assault of
the evil noumena, concealed in the bodies of the tourists.

CHAPTER XV

FLORENCE AND PISA

FROM Assisi we went to Florence by way of Arezzo, where
we dawdled for a few hours. We now felt rather aimless.
The Irish boy was a little dazed from the shocks he had received at Assisi. He felt that perhaps he was rather shallow
soil, that the seed which fell on him could not get its roots
down into the hard rock below, of scepticism or self-indul-
gence — he was not sure which. Still, he had to live according
to his nature, though he admitted that the pagan gods in him
needed redeeming, but not mutilating. He knew that there
were clergy who would tell him with a sweet evil smile that
he needed 'breaking on the Will of God'. He regards them
as devil-worshippers. He is certain that the will of the
Creative Nóos is that he should live healthily and happily.
The word 'blessed' used by Christ could more accurately be
translated as 'happy'. The Irish boy wants occasionally to
dine with the publicans, to have intelligent conversation with
women, to drink good wine, to love children, to take pleasure
in the flowers of the field and the natural world, to have nice
clothes and to play games on the Sabbath which was made
for man ; and he cannot see that any of these things are contrary to the gospels. He accepts that there may be occasions
when he will have to abandon one or all of them, and die like
the ermine. It seems only too likely, in our times. But now
he is young and healthy and he wants abundant life, and he
repeated that he could not honestly use prayers and hymns
which would only be suitable on the lips of those on the verge
of death.

So in Florence he kept away from churches, except Santa

Croce, where we went to see the tomb of Michelangelo. A bemused tourist who glanced casually at the inscription said to his wife : 'That's the tomb of Michelangelo Buonaparte'. The Irish boy felt that his own mind was approaching a similar confusion, and we went up to Fiesole to sit in the quiet of the Roman theatre, to let the blood descend from our brains, which we felt had been violating the conditions of our search. Also we wanted, watching the sunlight on the hills of Tuscany, to free our nerves from the vibrations of the motor bicycles, which apparently held races outside our rooms in the small hours of the morning. But habit is strong, and we could not keep out of the little museum of early Florentine painting. Here the Irish boy was cheered by a picture of God the Father as a strong young man of about thirty with a brown beard, a repudiation of the idea that the potent Creator of all things was senile, his hair white with approaching death, his nostrils hungry for the smell of young blood to renew his vitality.

We also went to the Fransciscan monastery on the Etruscan hill, where the same little friar has been showing round the tourists for thirty-five years. His activity has become almost frenzied. 'Have you seen the museum ?' 'One minute, please !' 'Have you seen the cloister?' he asks in English of bewildered French and Italian tourists, shoving them willy-nilly into these places, while he thrusts into their hands a slip of paper on which is printed the Benediction of S. Francis, efficacious in every sort of temptation. We calculated that he must have given away about 1,000,000 of these blessings, a curious row of noughts. In the cloisters are the birds of S. Francis, but they are in a cage.

On the terrace outside the convent we saw an incident which helped to restore a little that state of mind, or stimulation of the heart which was necessary to the Irish boy's search. It was very slight. A woman was standing there with her son and her daughter, a beautiful girl of sixteen. They were well dressed and had the appearance of belonging to the more educated social strata. An old beggar woman came along and they gave her money. She stood talking to them for a few minutes, and then said something which amused them. The girl laughed, and with an impulsive gesture took the old woman's brown and wrinkled hand in both her own, and held it for a moment affectionately. It was hard to imagine an English girl of the same class, whatever her feeling, showing such spontaneous kindness, such a sense of common humanity with the poor. It was the incident of S. Francis and the leper in the milder terms of the twentieth century.

We did not stay long in Florence, as the sponges with which we are fitted to absorb 'culture' were saturated. Our finger-tips refused to tingle any more, even at Botticelli's Venus, or Benvenuto's statues on the top floor of the Bargello. So we went to Pisa, where, someone told us, we could bathe from a sandy beach about twenty minutes away. We spent two days at Marina di Pisa, going there each morning in the electric train. When waiting for it the Italians sit on the edge of the low platform with their feet on the line. At Salerno we saw a woman at a level crossing push up the (to us) sacred barrier, just let down, and walk across the line with her baby, and we wondered how on earth they existed under Fascist rule.

On the third day we could no longer keep away from the Piazza dei Miracoli, with its group of three buildings which is surely the most beautiful in all Italy, and therefore in all the world. We went there in the evening, and the ancient marble was bathed in honey-gold light. Beyond, above the wall of the Campo Santo, was the line of the purple hills. It was like an illuminated background to the saints in Paradise, and it seemed as if there must really be some miraculous legend of its origin — perhaps that the Blessed Virgin, seeing the boy Christ sitting idle in one of those moments when the aware-ness of his destiny grew in him, told him : 'If you've no-thing to do, sit down and draw a temple', and he drew the cathedral of Pisa. For here there is some suggestion of the East, due to the fact that the Pisan merchants who had it built had acquired their riches through trading in Eastern countries. The effect of its being an illumination is increased not only by the expanses of gold over the doorway, but by its all being a little out of drawing. The cathedral as well as the leaning tower has an irregularity which makes it look as if it had been designed freehand. Nowhere can there be any more mysterious and yet serene creation by men's hands, not even the double basilica at Assisi, where the story of the saint flowers with its roots in the gospel story below. At S. Giorgio in Velabro, in spite of the echo of the hymns to the Light, there is a touch of sadness, as they followed the sufferings of the catacombs. But at S. Francesco and at Pisa the Christian religion has flowered in innocence and perfect beauty. The Christian noumena have found their true expression, and without them these churches could not have been built.

In the Campo Santo the frescoes of Benozzo Gozzoli, covering the vast walls of the cloister, were destroyed in the war by the lead from the burning roof. The saints in Paradise, the gardens, and the farms were blotted out. But one panel survives, showing the fiends in hell. The evil noumena had protected their own.

After dinner, by the rather *opéra-bouffe* statue of Victor Emanuel near the station, we saw something which may explain what we think of as irreverence. Some children were playing hide-and-seek, using the base of the statue as 'home'. Three young men were sitting on its steps engaged in serious discussion. The children at intervals dashed shrieking through them, calling out some word like 'gumba!' as they touched the base of the statue. It appeared that the Italians have not our intolerance towards any nuisance. They continue with their own activities and it does not occur to them that those of other people are an obstruction that it is possible to avoid.

The young men do not tell the children to go away ; the children do not find another base where the intervening bodies of the young men do not increase their chances of being caught. So the sightseers and gossipers in church are not irreverent. They are just doing something else. At the correct moment they make a gesture, as if they were talking in the street and a friend passed, with whom at another time they might be intimately engaged, and they take off their hats without interrupting their conversation.

The Irish boy accepted this explanation, but without much interest. He had to return to England in ten days. Now at the beginning of August it was very hot, and he wanted to go to a place right on the sea, where he could spend the whole time bathing. We took out the map, and fixed on S. Margherita-Ligure, which often had looked so inviting from the train.

On the way we asked him if he had found the object of his search. He said :

'Well, I think I have a clearer idea of what I've been looking for, but the difficulty is where to find it. Christ is a noumenon, existing through all time, the Logos in the beginning ; whether for five thousand or a million years before me doesn't matter. Its senseless rows of noughts — a game for theologians. Then at last in the fullness of time he became a phenomenon, to show man the image of his own perfection, which we call God. He was a phenomenon, not an intellect. He was the jewel in the cradle, the sparkling boy, the noble man, shedding from his very nature, not as the result of the processes of his mind, wisdom and kindness and healing wherever he moved ; and finally he was killed by the Calibans who could only bear their own imperfect faces in the glass, killed like the ermine because of his perfection. His function was Being, and his wisdom came from his heart and not his head. He showed us how to live again with innocence and pleasure in the natural world. Because of all this we adore him, not because we're frightened of hell, or think we'll drive a bargain with the Almighty and get a crown of glory laid by for us as the result of a respectable life. I heard a Presbyterian minister say that the three temptations were really three periods of intensive study, each lasting seven years. If it were so he would have come out of them, not the Glorious Son of God, but short-sighted, stooping, peevish, full of pedantic references and rather like the man with the *New Statesman* in his pocket; and he would have written all his teaching down, most carefully and explicitly in legal language. But he said: "Woe to you lawyers," and he just lived, he just *was*. You might as well try to draw up a legal moral system from looking at the Ephebe of Subiaco. Apart from the necessary myth, he was god from the beginning in his perfection. If he was not that he was just a dreary candidate for the ethical society.

'Very well. Then the marvellous period in which he was a phenomenon came to an end. He had revealed himself to man, almost like a process of nature; and we know that it is difficult and dangerous to think separately of God and nature. He revealed himself to man and left man to do the rest, as nature itself leaves it to man to draw his life from her. Then S. Paul came along, and not having known him, but seeing the results of his teaching in the Christians he was butchering, was convinced it was the truth. He drew it all up in his own version of the myth, killing the living image at once, and putting the focus of our attention beyond the grave, to the cash rewards.

'The Acts of the Apostles was the first Christian book, then the Gospels were written to fix the myth of Pauline religion. But they were written by men who had known · Christ, or from direct information given by those men. So in them we have the pure honey, but even they were coloured slightly by the prevalent Pauline doctrine. But Christ is a noumenon, an object of intuitive apprehension, and where

in the gospels we find things inconsistent with the perfection
that is shown in other places, our intuitive apprehension dis-
cards those things, and we are left with the pure honey. The
idea that he can be understood by the intellect alone is responsible for all the shadows and the shivers, the Inquisition
fires, the vicious Calvinism, all the hell-born accretions which
have stuck to the Pauline varnish and hidden his Face from
us for nearly two thousand years.

'But the clergy love the Pauline accretions — whether
they are Roman or Anglican or Protestant. They love the
idea of eternal hell. Even if they don't believe the punishment
is burning, they insist on its endlessness. Think of the young
girl who catches her dress in a gas fire and dies from the burns.
It is so awful we can hardly bear to think of it. Her beautiful
life is destroyed, but at least her sufferings are over in a few
hours, or perhaps a few days. But the clergy insist that God
is going to condemn people to those sufferings or something
as bad for ever — not for a day, nor a year but for eternity,
endless rows of noughts. And he is our loving Father!
Well, really . . .

'When Anthony Froude wrote a book in which a character
said he could not worship a god who "kept a hell prison
house" his name was removed from his college, and his
father, a fox-hunting archdeacon, turned him out penniless,
and Charles Kingsley who had given him shelter turned him
out at his own father's request — all Anglican clergy. A
Victorian dean, after reading a book of Higher Criticism,
exclaimed : "No devil? No hell? Horrible! Horrible!"
I have known young Catholic converts furious at the idea
that there was no eternal hell, and there was a correspondence
in an Anglo-Catholic newspaper saying that to deny hell was
not "Catholic". It's not for me to tell them what they should
believe or do, but if they ask us to come and join them, we
can tell them why we don't. When you first meet Christians
you are drawn towards them by their nice smell of honey,

but soon you get a whiff of the chemicals, and even now and then of scorching human flesh. And yet the awful thing — or perhaps it's a good thing — is that they are the only people absolutely committed to the good. If the world for the last fifty years had been under the direction of the popes, from S. Pius X onwards, it's obvious that we would be living in peace, with all wealth turned to the benefit of mankind instead of exploded. No violence would be done to innocent creation, to quiet islands, and God's fish in the sea, and we would not be living under the threat of extermination. The Church must still contain Christ or it would not be so opposed by those who want to destroy the human soul, and it has today as many martyrs as in the time of the Quattro Coronati. Even the princes of the Church are martyred, like the apostles. But though the Church holds Christ, it is as a prisoner, like the Hermes in the Court of the Belvedere, and when they show us his Face, it is covered with a mask.'

The Irish boy sat silent and despondent for a while, then he looked out with anticipation at those little beaches, with their sunbathers and bright umbrellas and bathing toys, which dazzle us suddenly between the tunnels west of Spezia. His mood changed.

'I expect I've been trying to use my brains,' he said a little more cheerfully, 'and that was forbidden by the rules. If a clever Jesuit were in this carriage, he could knock my arguments flat. And if a clever scientist were here, he too could knock them flat from the other side. Yet one of them would have to be wrong. So what use is the intellect alone? Descartes, you say, divorced science from conscience, and Rabelais said that when science became divorced from the conscience of mankind, mankind was doomed. He might have said the same of theology, which also has been divorced from conscience, the intuitive apprehension of the noumena, and has relied on the letter alone, which killeth. This carriage must be full of the devils of the Third Temptation. It's as hot as hell. Why do they have red-velvet cushions in this climate ?'

We may have appeared a little dissatisfied at not hearing some more positive result from his pilgrimage, as he said :

'But thank you very much for helping me. Perhaps something may come of it some day, and anyhow it has made our holiday more interesting. Santa Margherita ! Here we are ! Oh, isn't the sea blue ? And all the arches are round, thank Heaven !'

CHAPTER XVI

THE LIGHT ON THE SEA

SANTA MARGHERITA-LIGURE was like a painting by Dufy. Everything was blue and fun. We went straight down to bathe where the sea stretched placid and shimmering towards Africa. The bathers were nearly naked and a golden brown, but they had little blue enamel medals of the Madonna round their necks. Before they went into the water they dipped in their hands and crossed themselves three times. We thought at first that they must have mistaken the Mediterranean for a holy water stoup, and then realized that it is the holy water of our civilization. They live naturally and unconsciously in the two Stories. From near by the water-skiers set out, skimming gloriously over the waves like souls set free, the modern equivalent of the boy on the dolphin.

In the town the baroque churches with their onion spires, and their interiors sparkling with gold and every kind of prettiness, exist in their own right, and have not superimposed themselves on more venerable beauties. There are no 'tormentose nostalgie del divino' and even where the images bleed we feel that they are really Mrs. Siddons.

In the evening the town was like a stage set for musical comedy. We dined out of doors, overlooking the harbour, and expected that at any moment a man might appear on a balcony and sing to the accompaniment of an orchestra which was playing in a sort of garden-restaurant. This did not happen, but a religious procession came along the street, carrying a number of large crucifixes ornamented with elaborate gold filigree. The huge swaying figures looked rather dreadful, especially when they had to be lowered under the electric-light wires, but they did not provoke any reaction from the Irish boy, who had declared that for the next ten days he had no intention of using his brains in any way, excepting to order his dinner, and then they would be under the direction of his stomach.   The orchestra stopped playing as the procession passed.

Every day we spent in and out of the water, and lunched under ceilings of hanging grapes.   Nowhere was anything but pleasure, and yet the people did not seem to have less contact with the noumena than in the holy places of Assisi and Rome.   In the gilded churches there was always a handful of people come to place themselves under their protection ; every evening the Maddalenas loudly chanted their rosaries ; the little girls made their flying curtsies, and the *putti* occupied themselves fussily in the sanctuary.   On Sunday at the sung mass the cathedral was packed, but in this gaudy brilliance the congregation was as quiet and reverent as in the austerity of S. Anselmo.   The young priest, with a kind and honest face, walked about the town with his crew of children.

On the ninth day of this wise but brainless life, our last in Italy, we climbed the hill above the town to the west, walking up steep and rugged pathways and along narrow tracks between the terraces where the afternoon sun slanted through the olives.   We passed little farm-houses, hidden amongst their vines, heavy with purple grapes, and fruit trees laden with pears and apples.   Ripe plums squashed under our feet. The little gardens with zinnias and tomatoes were irrigated through bamboo pipes, and the silence was only broken by the trickling water.

'It is like something in the *Odyssey*,' said the Irish boy. 'This is the eternal pattern of life for mankind, each with his own vine and his own fig tree.   This is how we should live, in the enclosed garden of the natural world, in scale with our surroundings, worshipping the noumena of the place, giving them occasionally gifts of fruit and putting flowers between the feet of Hermes. This is the paradise that we really long for.'

Soon we came on to the piazza of Nozzarego, and as we did so a procession came out of the church. They carried a statue of the Virgin, surrounded with flowers and candles and banners. They were all enjoying themselves. No one was particularly solemn, and a boy whose cassock was too short for him, showing his comic white socks, turned round to gossip with another behind him. The procession moved away along the track between the sunlit olive trees, and again the afternoon fell into silence.

It was the Feast of the Assumption, which in his periods of over-cerebration had given the Irish boy so much concern. When we reminded him of this he brushed it aside.

'That sort of thing doesn't matter,' he said. 'These people are living in the Story. They are living the best sort of natural life, but illuminated by the noumena. They are the sort of people from whom exhausted humanity always has to renew itself.'

We walked down by a different way, past more Odyssean farms. From the bend of the lane we saw the promontory of Portofino, sleeping on the flat and vivid sea. Below us two water-skiers behind the same boat were weaving ecstatic curves, and in the delight of the flesh seeming to transcend it. We had come into what was surely the most complete paradise possible on this earth, equal to the heights of Ravello, beyond the dreams of Beato Angelico. And somehow it seemed that the Assumption of the Virgin was connected with all this delight, that the material beauty was raised into heaven, in a way which we who do not use our minds could feel but not understand.

In the evening we began to collect our things, ready to leave on the next day, but after dinner the Irish boy went out for a walk. In a short time he returned, his face alight with excitement.

'You must come out,' he said, 'it's marvellous.'

THE LIGHT ON THE SEA

We replied that we wanted to pack, that the afternoon's walk had been a perfect end to our tour, and we did not want to see anything more.

'But this is much better,' he exclaimed. 'The sea! It's a miracle!'

He was so insistent that reluctantly we went with him down to the harbour. Almost as far as we could see, beyond the point of Rapallo and away to the mole on our right, the water was shimmering with the soft golden light of thousands of candles, floating in cardboard holders. Men in boats were rowing about lighting more candles and setting them on the water. The effect was indescribably lovely, the most beautiful form of illumination we have ever known.

The Irish boy said that the boat of the materialistic scientist could not float in that water. We suggested that perhaps it had capsized and he was drowned. The poor man finds his soul in the hands of the powers in which he does not believe. The evil noumena rush like a wind to a vacuum to fill his emptiness, while the good noumena, who do not understand English, and so are only aware of his desire to be honest and not of his intellectual statements, for the sake of this try to rescue him, and he finds himself the very battlefield of the war in heaven. His sufferings are appalling, but he will finally be delivered through our prayers and his own desire for honesty.

There is, however, another boat out there, and one far more menacing. We can just discern amongst those leaning over the side, trying to feel a tingling in their finger-tips, a man in a green jacket against which there is a white dot, which might be a weekly paper. He is, rather oddly, a guest on a millionaire's yacht, but the millionaire is also a Communist who hopes after the revolution to become a super-commissar owing to his great managerial efficiency, and so make little alteration in his way of life. He is at the moment engaged in smashing any small businesses and farms that remain, the units of English freedom and potential mirrors of

Bethlehem, a project equally dear to the heart of the man with the *New Statesman*. As neither of them have any conception of the Perfect Drawing, of the divine humanity which should inform our society, they are like a pair of architects with the most up-to-date equipment, a complete knowledge of strains and stresses, but with not the faintest idea of what a house should look like, or what kind of people should live in it.

The yacht pushed its way among the candles, swamping many of them, hiding the light of others from the shore, so that the owner could have a close-up of what only should be seen with worship from afar.

The Irish boy was horrified and distressed. There were angry tears in his eyes.

'I would rather be the poorest fisherman lighting those candles,' he said, 'than the owner of the yacht that is putting them out.'

From this statement it seemed that his search was rewarded. For he had, at the centre of his being, renounced the world; not the natural world, the enclosed garden which is our home, but the evil world which exploits it for the gratification of senseless lusts, of the tingling insulated from the heart, and of power and of pride.

At Paestum in May the earth was covered with flowers around the temple of Ceres, the mother of the fruitful earth and of our bodies. At Santa Margherita in August the sea was covered with light in honour of the Mother of Christ and of our souls. The two Stories, the Greek story and the Gospel story, the first redeemed by the second, had combined to meet his double nature, and in them, in spite of all stumbling-blocks, he will live and move and have his being.

THE END